Which stock market in Southeast Asia registered an unprecedented turnover of zero dollars, zero cents on a trading day in 1990?

What happened to Hongkong firm Turns Out All Right Co Ltd?

Which major Hongkong department store sold globular pieces of brown confection called Chocolate Negro Balls?

Who addressed a letter to a Hongkong stockbroking firm addressed to "Mr Dealing Room" and starting: "Dear Mr Room . . ."?

Why was the "Omni The Hongkong Hotel" renamed "Omen The Honking Hotel"?

The Secret Diaries of Lai See

By Nury Vittachi

Illustrations by Paul Best

Sub-editor: Kris Meland

PACIFIC CENTURY BOOKS

A South China Morning Post Book
Published by Pacific Century Books

Text: © Nury Vittachi 1991
Illustrations: © Paul Best 1991

ISBN 962-7290-01-7

Typeset by South China Morning Post Publishers Ltd

Printed by Leefung-Asco Printers, Hongkong

Pacific Century Books is a trading name of Hongkong-registered Pacific Century Film Co Ltd.

First Impression, November 1991
Second Impression, January 1992

CONTENTS

PREFACE

LAI SEE has many addicts, but there is no more compulsive reader than me. It is one of the sections of the newspaper I turn to first, not just because it brings a welcome injection of humour into the working day, but because, as Editor, I have to ensure that there is no risk of libel!

That whiff of danger is part of the character of Lai See. It is cheeky, scandalous, scurrilous and outrageous, without being malicious. Certainly it is not a column for the faint-hearted – good taste is not a speciality – but, thanks to the wit and excellent contacts of its editor, Nury Vittachi, it says more about Hongkong and its foibles than any other part of the newspaper on a daily basis. Like most good satirists and social observers, Nury is as uncomplimentary about the expats as he is about the locals.

This collection is the result of his initiative, and it is a tribute to the niche Lai See has established that there has been so much support for the project. I thank everyone who has helped to make it possible, and I hope it will make lots of money for the charities concerned.

Phillip Crawley
Editor
South China Morning Post

A WORD ABOUT OUR SPONSORS

GRATEFUL thanks go to the many Hongkong firms who have supported the publication of this book. Particular mention goes to John Yang and Jack Yang of LEEFUNG-ASCO PRINTERS, Len Kruse and the staff of CRESVALE GROUP OF COMPANIES, and Ted Thomas and the staff of CORPORATE COMMUNICATIONS. These firms provided the impetus leading to the production of the first edition of this book.

To Mr X
who knows who he is
which is more than I do

AUTHOR'S NOTE:

Hongkong is not so much a place, as an economic principle which has taken flesh and set itself up on earth as The Free Market Incarnate.

The human repercussions of this frequently pop up as bizarre tales in the Lai See column of the *South China Morning Post*.

In this book, the sources of the information have been sketched back in, to give readers a peek at the workings of the newsroom.

For the sake of flow, I have occasionally adjusted dates and places, and combined different sources into single entities.

But the stories themselves are true, and Five-Finger Wu, Big Swinging Richard and the gang are as real as anyone in this crazy city.

N.V. October 1991.

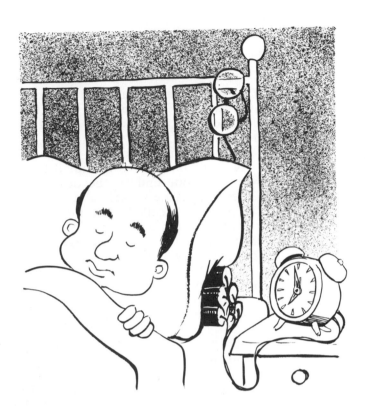

WOKE up. Looked at the clock. Realised it was much too early to rise. Think about it in around ninety minutes — the beginning of cocktail hour.

Suddenly realised that this was not just a new day, new month and new year, but A NEW DECADE. Important to start it as one means to go on.

Determined to get up and achieve something today.

Unfortunately, fell straight back to sleep.

Never mind. It surely does no good to overdo things at the start of what will clearly be a tumultuous decade for Hongkong.

THE trouble started as soon as the first day — or at least, the first reasonably lengthy period of unbroken consciousness — of the year was underway.

Got up, switched on the radio.

Nothing but static. Twiddled the dial all the way from one end to the other. Not a single English-speaking voice.

Then we recalled that the authorities had recently altered all the radio frequencies, with the result that English-language services were no longer widely available.

The official reason was "enhanced efficiency in frequency distribution". Hmm.

Tried to phone the office.

Got a recorded message reminding us that in the early hours of December 30, the Hongkong Telephone Company had changed all the numbers.

The occasion had been dubbed "Easy Dialling Day" by the phone company in what we can only surmise must have been an uncharacteristic burst of corporate "humour".

Dialled six digits. The recorded message replied: "Please dial seven digits."

Dialled seven digits. The recorded message replied: "Please dial seven digits."

Hit the body of the phone several times with a blunt instrument, to wit, the handset. The recorded message replied: "Please dial seven digits."

Shocked after this betrayal by the familiar instrument on which we depend for our livelihood, we made our way to the haven of old-fashioned habits: the Foreign Correspondents' Club of Hongkong.

"The usual, Johnnie," we said.

"New system, sir. Please hand over your computer membership card, before you order drink," replied barman Johnnie.

Damn and blast us if a computer hadn't taken over the FCC on the SAME weekend!

GOT talking about this bizarre concerted technological assault with a secretive Hongkong businessman, who we will call Luddite Lo.

He claims that all these sudden hi-tech adjustments introduced *en masse,* are part of a secret plot in which Beijing and London work together to "tighten" control on Hongkong before the big day.

Sounds a bit far-fetched, we know, but things have undeniably changed since the "incident" of June 4 last year.

WE were mulling over the prospect of ever more having breakfast without our much-missed Radio Three chit-chat, when we got a call from south side businessman Rolf Hess.

He said he had recently given away his illegal cordless telephone and bought a licensed one from CSL.

Now he had discovered that whenever he talks on it from his home on the 16th floor of his block in Repulse Bay, his private conversations can be heard with bell-like clarity by his friend who has a radio on floor 10.

If you strategically located yourself at the right place in his tower block, you would be able to eavesdrop on ALL the cordless telephones in the vicinity just by re-tuning your radio.

"Hours of fun. Who needs English language broadcasting?" asked Mr Hess.

AN hour later the phone rang. It was Rolf Hess again.

"You had better not print the name of my block in your column. Otherwise everyone will come and listen to me on their radios," he said in a worried voice.

It is a pity Mr Hess has no ambitions to go into the broadcasting business.

Thursday 4 JANUARY

GOT to the office to find our editor-cum-headline-writer, "the Texas Chainsaw Sub", in a foul mood.

"Gloom mounting," he growled unhappily. "I've just learned that Harry Ramsden's isn't coming."

We gave him our renowned blank look.

"Harry Ramsden's Fish and Chip Restaurant. It's the best fish 'n chip shop in Yorkshire — and that means the world," grumbled "Chainsaw" Charlie.

Last year the firm considered Hongkong an ideal place for a branch in Asia. But now, following the "event" of June 4, the superlative crispy cod had been re-routed to Singapore, he lamented.

"See what you have done, Li Peng," howled the wounded Brit. "The most serious repercussions of June 4 are only now beginning to emerge."

The business news editor "chipped in" with a comment that one could get a portion of Harry Ramsden's through a stockbroker, as the chippie had just been floated on Britain's third stock market.

"Quite right," we said. "Or if you were really desperate you could try DHL."

Chainsaw failed to find this amusing.

Friday 5 JANUARY

HAVING an idle hour between appointments in the morning, we spent some time twiddling around with the radio trying to find some English language broadcasting.

We really miss the friendly English voices.

Even strolled around a couple of residential blocks in the hopes of picking up some cordless phone calls.

All to no avail.

Tempted to drive down to Repulse Bay and listen into Rolf Hess's private telephone calls.

LATER in the afternoon, Mr Hess called to tell us that the engineer from CSL had taken away his cordless phone to see if they can stop him entertaining the neighbourhood.

Good thing we didn't waste our time heading off to the south side of the island earlier today.

Saturday
6
JANUARY

ON this bright winter's morning, we got talking to a Hongkong-based chemicals executive for whom "Easy" Dialling Day had almost prompted a major personal crisis of confidence.

He was stranded at Jakarta Airport on January 2 and decided to call his office in Hongkong.

The clerk said to him: "But which side is it? Hongkong or Kowloon?"

"There is no longer any distinction between the two," he replied. "The numbering system has changed."

She refused to accept this. "You MUST have an area code," she insisted.

He saw that he would have to explain the whole business of Easy Dialling Day, so he did. He saw the light of understanding burst forth in her eyes.

She said: "Aha! Now it is 1990, Hongkong has already gone back to China. There is no longer Hongkong or Kowloon."

At that stage, he realised that the operator was

going to use 86, the IDD code for China instead of 852, the code for Hongkong.

The businessman was about to remonstrate, but something stopped him.

After all, he had been out of Hongkong for a number of days, and hadn't seen a newspaper recently.

"Did she know something I didn't?" he asked himself.

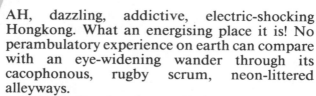

AH, dazzling, addictive, electric-shocking Hongkong. What an energising place it is! No perambulatory experience on earth can compare with an eye-widening wander through its cacophonous, rugby scrum, neon-littered alleyways.

So what if pedestrian traffic is so heavy that a short stroll leaves you badly bruised?

So what if air-conditioners urinate on your head at every corner?

So what if construction projects elbow you onto the roads, where rude taxi-drivers nudge you into "repair" holes (the only permanent parts of the cityscape)?

So what if the air is so polluted that you have to chew before inhaling? Don't you like to see what you are breathing?

No. One can never be bored in Hongkong, because nothing stays the same for any length of time here.

That ethereal transience applies to everything, from the 20-year built-in obsolescence of the buildings, right up to the ownership of the entire territory, as the bickering of our guardians, China and Britain, keeps reminding us.

As we write this, we are sitting at our breakfast table in Causeway Bay, with our morning coffee and the *South China Morning Post* in front of us.

We gaze out into a breathtaking panorama showing an angular skyline of metallic towers, jostling precariously between the glittering water and the distant craggy hills of . . . Good Lord! What's that in the newspaper?

A new reclamation in the harbour? Developments to BLOCK SEAVIEWS from present waterfront properties? Harbour to be 50 per cent of original width?

Damn and blast the place! Can't they jolly well leave things alone for five minutes?

Monday 8 JANUARY

DIDN'T go to the office, but went straight to Exchange Square, where we had an early lunch at Brown's Wine Bar with an American corporate financier, who we know as Fast Buck.

He says that the Hongkong economy will go faster and faster as we approach 1997, rather than slow down.

"This is because bosses have now earned enough to buy passports out of here, so managers and under-managers are trying to follow the same path," he said. "We are about to undergo a period of brain drain-inspired money-mania, in which people will do ANYTHING to make a buck," he said.

That's why there is so much business activity: construction, street-hawking, junk mail, gambling, telephone marketing.

One sign will be that whenever people see a profit opportunity, such as a new property development for sale, they will rush in, despite the fact that there are only seven years left before 1997.

"It's like Pavlov's dogs," he added, obscurely.

We agreed to look for evidence for this, although what it has to do with a popular meringue dessert we have no idea.

WHEN he got to the office, there was a package on our desk. The Hotel Conrad, shortly to open in Hongkong, had sent *Lai See* a diary.

It included all the major national holidays all around the world, including:

"December 25. Christmas Day. Conrad N. Hilton's birthday."

Surely the chap's name was Jesus H. Christ?

THE first call of the day was from a reader moaning on the phone that a local firm was sending him junk faxes.

"Everyone gets them," we said.

"But the thing this lot are advertising is fax paper," he replied.

How fiendishly clever. Clearly, if it sends out enough of these, people will have to buy new paper to replenish their supply.

The people at Star Liaison of Pedder Street have curiously forgotten to include their own fax number on their material.

"This is so we junk fax victims cannot get our own back," alleged the recipient.

No. Surely that would be just too devious for words?

We called Star Liaison manager Wilson Wu to ask.

Lai See: Why do you not write your own fax number on your faxes?

Mr Wu: Because we usually use the telephone for contact with customers.

Lai See: Why?

Mr Wu: Because we usually use the telephone for contact with customers.

Lai See: But why? Do you not think faxes are a good way to communicate?

Mr Wu: (Long pause.) Sorry?

Lai See: Why don't you use your fax number on your faxes?

(Even longer pause follows.)

Mr Wu: Whose fax number?

Lai See: Your fax number.

Mr Wu: You mean why don't we use our fax number on the faxes?

Lai See: Yes, that is the question.

Mr Wu: Because the fax number is not used.

Lai See: But why?

Mr Wu: Because it is NOT used.

We conceded at this point. Life is short.

SEEN in a trade magazine:

"Staff Wanted for Korean Association of Profreaders."

Clearly the need is urgent.

Wednesday 10 JANUARY

HOW curious. The barrow boy, who for months has been selling oranges on the corner of King's Road and Oil Street in North Point, has suddenly moved upmarket — he has switched to mink coats.

At least he says they are mink.

On the other hand, that small group of grey squirrels in the northwest corner of Victoria Park have not been seen for several days.

He was doing a roaring trade, and talk about zero overheads.

A fine example of Hongkong quick-reaction entrepreneurialism.

We picked up a coat for an aunt on the way to work.

Chainsaw Charlie was not impressed. "Fur cheat cons hack," he said.

We admit the Park'N Shop plastic bag that it came in doesn't quite have the cachet of Prestige Furs of the Regent.

WONG and Ouyang, a North Point architectural firm, is advertising for CADs:

"This is an excellent opportunity to those motivated candidates who wish to further their CAD careers."

Curious that such sexist attitudes are still fostered in these allegedly enlightened times.

NOTED that the World Toy Fair opens at the Hongkong Convention Centre tomorrow.

A few hours spent there should relax the brain, which has been rather overheated recently.

RELAX the brain?

Not a bit of it. We forgot how gruesome are the things that entertain children these days.

Oozy green slime and horror film merchandise filled the World Toy Fair.

Along with the traditional Frankenstein masks at the Winmento Co stall was a mask of Freddy Krueger.

He is the disfigured pervert with blades attached to his fingers from the film series *Nightmare On Elm Street.*

"His life's work is gratuitous mutilation," a toy industry official helpfully explained.

We learned that Universal Matchbox had been in trouble for producing a "Freddy" doll.

Can there be any activity for which children can use them, other than the molestation of Barbie dolls, made by arch-rival toymaker Mattel?

FOUND an anonymous gift of a bottle of scotch on our desk when we got back to the office.

BACK to the toy fair this morning to discover

another strange development: there is a whole sub-section of the industry in Hongkong churning out plastic fast food.

We are not employing metaphors, but talking about burgers in which every gherkin slice is provided in plastic. A big seller is a "McDonald's Hot Apple Pie" that doubles as a flute.

Gazing at these was a chap we vaguely knew from the fast food industry. "Many of these plastic fast food products look amazingly like the real thing," he said.

We replied: "Has it occurred to anyone that they probably taste identical as well?"

Why can't fast food people see the funny side of their industry?

THERE was a big turn-out at a press conference for visiting publisher Erich Ulrich, of Vienna magazine *Austria Business and Economy.*

We asked our local counterparts why they had flocked. "Because of the prefixes," one said.

"His full name must be Mr Extra-Rich Ultra-Rich."

NO clues yet as to the identity of the mysterious bottle-of-scotch deliverer.

Saturday
13
JANUARY

CAREFULLY checked our person to make sure we were not carrying freebies of any sort, and went off to visit the offices of the ICAC, or Independent Commission Against Corruption.

If someone tells you that the shady world of the ICAC is like a jungle, he does not mean that it is dark and impenetrable. He means you can't move for plants.

The Murray Road office of the Independent Commission Against Corruption has almost disappeared under the weight of exotic foliage.

These ladies and gentlemen, known for their

crack-of-dawn dispensing of full-face paper-bag headgear, are shortly to have their annual cocktail party for sources. They traditionally line the corridors with neat rows of little kumquat bushes.

But this year they have something that looks like the Forest of Birnham Wood doing a final rehearsal in the corridor before setting off to Macbeth's castle.

You cannot pass anyone in the corridor without getting a mouthful of foliage, unless you have a machete.

Imagine having to negotiate these corridors wearing a paper bag over your head!

Another reason to stay on the straight and narrow. Must remember to return that bottle of scotch. But to whom?

LOOKING forward to a trip tomorrow on a pleasure-junk to a romantic blue-water bay off one of Hongkong's 230-plus little-used islets.

Monday 15 JANUARY

GOT to the office feeling distinctly unwell this morning, after spending a torrid day yesterday swimming near our junk, which was bobbing around in what appeared to be the main sewage effluent stream for the whole of South China.

THE first call of the day was from Ms Jane Ram, a freelance writer living on Lamma Island, who admitted to being a fellow techno-phobe.

"I've been trying to rid myself of the Curse of the Phantom Credit Card Statement for months," she said.

It all started when the computer billed her HK$150 as a renewal fee for a card she never used. "So I cut up the card and returned it, explaining that I did not feel I should pay the HK$150," she said.

The computer, in a display of humanity that would have done many human bank managers proud, agreed. It cancelled the HK$150 and then charged ITSELF the interest on the sum.

This left it owing Ms Ram nine cents. Now, every month without fail, it sends her a computer-print out informing her of this.

The trouble is, she cannot cancel the balance by buying something for nine cents, because she no longer has a card. She cut it up and returned it in paragraph three, remember?

"I am cursed with getting this statement every month for the rest of my life," she said.

Whoever thought up the term Artificial Intelligence has never been on a computer's mailing list.

THE first time that we met Five-Finger Wu (so called because of the number of digits he has on each hand), he had already started his now-landmark investigation of Chinese medicine.

He was an American-educated Chinese, convinced that somewhere existed a piece of Chinese culture crying out to be transferred to the rich West.

And he was going to be the middleperson who would make millions doing it.

His latest discovery was underwear produced in Fujian province that could prevent sexually-transmitted diseases.

The HK$50 unisex knickers contain a little-known Chinese fibre that kills off all known germs.

"They'll be the hottest product of the 1990s, the days of AIDS, herpes, VD and so on," he enthused.

We wanted to write a major feature about them but Chainsaw Charlie was skeptical.

"Why not put superglue on ordinary knickers,

so you can't get them off? That would help stop sexually transmitted diseases," he scoffed.

Wednesday 17 JANUARY

TODAY there was a tribunal hearing on air routes between Hongkong and Vietnam, and it included a fascinating revelation.

Air Vietnam has been paying its share of joint ventures in seafood, according to Air Hongkong consultant Mr Frank Skilbeck.

We can just picture the negotiations: "Why don't you Boeing reps just try some of these delicious prawns? And we'll throw in some Honest Linh's genuine Shark's Fin-Like Soup if you'll give us the 747-400 Big Top version with the individual video units."

The return of the barter system will put those hi-tech usurers, the credit card agencies, in their place.

AGREED to have lunch at a new restaurant in the recently-opened Grand Hyatt hotel.

The place was littered with large pot plants. Could not help but peer into each one as we passed.

Until we work out who to return the scotch to, we cannot be too careful about the latest corruption-swooping methods of the ICAC.

A TALE we heard over lunch indicated that the brain drain is also a linguist drain, since bilingual people are first to get passports.

A waitress at a five-star hotel in Hongkong interrupted the breakfast of two hotel guests.

"I am having a bath at 10," she said cheerfully, and waltzed off.

She returned again and smiled helpfully at the diners. "I am having a bath at 10," she reminded them, then returned to repeat the statement a third time.

As 10 am approached they began to get excited. Is it normal to make announcements about one's personal hygiene in Hongkong? Was their presence around the tub required as part of a bizarre Hongkong ritual?

At zero hour, it was revealed that she meant: "I am opening the bar at 10."

BUMPED into the Lamma Looker at the FCC. He is a correspondent who likes to observe Hongkong life from his solitary vantage point on Lamma island.

He said he had been thinking about the Vietnamese trying to swap seafood for aeroplanes.

"They could offer jumbo prawns," he said.

BUSINESS news editor Nick Thompson returned sniggering from lunch, saying he had learned full details of The Super Strong Beer Incident. His tale shed some light on the characteristics of a certain Hongkong expat group.

The New Territories brewery accidentally sent 30 kegs of Carlsberg Special Brew to customers labelled as normal beer.

(People who drink Special Brew as if it were ordinary beer are not recommended to then perform complicated actions, such as moving any part of their bodies.)

Regulars at a bar in rural Sai Kung rang to complain that there was something wrong with their beer.

Carlsberg staff realised a mistake had been made, and traced the rest of the consignment to a pub in Tsim Sha Tsui favoured by Hongkong's Australian population.

The reaction there was different.

"They said the consumption rate had miraculously soared and there wasn't a drop to reclaim," said a Carlsberg executive.

Friday 19 JANUARY

FAST Buck met us at the Luk Yu Tea House with what he claims was evidence of growing money mania.

He was referring to a firm in Fa Yuen Street, which offered a remarkably wide-ranging service.

"Just look at the letterhead," he said. It read:

"Dominic's Art Gallery Co, manufacturer, importer, exporter, commission agents of fine oil paintings, and ultrasonic rodent and insect eliminators."

It did not seem irrational to us.

Once hard-working Dominic has manufactured and exported his fine oil paintings, and imported whatever he imports, and collected his commission on everything, it would be annoying to find his goods riddled with rodents and insects.

Vertical integration, they call it at Harvard Business School.

Saturday 20 JANUARY

THE office is usually deadly dull on a Saturday, but there was some important news today: another source of English language broadcasting has disappeared from the airwaves.

People in Repulse Bay will find that they can no longer tune into the personal calls of unwilling broadcaster Rolf Hess.

A team of CSL engineers arrived at his flat to sort out why his private phone calls were shooting up the ratings chart on his neighbours' radios.

Unfortunately, they could not completely prevent his conversations being tuned into.

Instead, with a masterstroke of inspiration,

they fiddled about with the innards of the phone so that recipients of his conversations get it at the same level of quality that many people now pick up English language Radio Three. That is, too fuzzy to listen to or enjoy.

"I am no longer attractive for those who prefer FM quality," enthused Mr Hess.

THIS weekend, we were most careful to tell the junk skipper to avoid sewage outflow areas.

Instead, he parked us in a massive free-floating island of supermarket bags and other rubbish (it was at least two acres, we swear) somewhere along the coast of Lantau.

THE Monday morning mail contained clear evidence of the growing money-mania in Hongkong. It was a photograph which captured the marketing spirit of Hongkong in the 1990s.

It shows a reader's three children standing with Santa Claus on the streets of Kowloon, with the colourful Christmas Lights of the Tsim Sha Tsui East hotels in the background.

Santa Claus is holding a sack of condoms, packets of which he has cheerfully distributed to the children.

"I know people would do anything to make a sale, but this really takes the cake," a parent told us.

We traced the Readi-Skin condoms to the US Secure Co in the New Territories.

"This is one of our marketing strategies," said Mr Sin Yip-keung, marketing manager.

He did not want us to think they were just doing it to make money. Oh no. "We are supporting the Prevent AIDS campaign from the Health Department," he explained earnestly.

Hmm. We suppose that's all right then.

BOOKED lunch at the Peperone, a Sichuan restaurant in Kornhill Plaza, for a meeting with a lady who works for American Express opposite our office.

The spicy food here is blisteringly hot enough to inspire various psychological reactions, including, or so it feels, making smoke come out of one's ears.

But we still can't work out why its lunch menu talks about steamed bums.

Decided to stick to the set menu, for fear of embarrassing our lady fellow-diner.

TURNED up at the Government land auction and spotted half a dozen umptillionaires in the audience.

This is where we will see some real wheeling and dealing, we thought.

But no. The Hongkong Government could hardly give the stuff away.

This definitely blows a hole in Fast Buck's theory about increasing property speculation. What went wrong?

It was generally agreed that the problem was that property king Robert Ng of Sino Land was out of town. Honestly, you'd think the Government would realise the need to check Mr Ng's whereabouts before they organise these things.

The almost total lack of bidding for two of the lots made the audience extremely uncomfortable.

As the property man next to us commented: "I wanted desperately to scratch my head, but I knew I would have ended up owning a small industrial plot in Yuen Long."

There were a number of mysterious agents there who would not say who they were bidding on behalf of.

Is this the beginning of the end for the Hongkong economy?

THE Lunar New Year holiday feeling is in the air.

The unmistakeable signals are present everywhere. No, we are not talking about peach blossom and miniature orange trees.

We are talking about the vast amount of begging letters asking firms to donate prizes for staff parties.

These are supposed to be sent to individual contacts at wealthy firms which will not miss handing over a spare computer or two to be given away during the festival.

But this year, organisers seem to have gone through their name-card files and sent them to everyone they have ever met.

David Gunson, a lawyer based in Prince's Building, Central, rang up and told us he was fuming at having received one of these.

It was sent by big advertising firm McCann-Erickson to Craigin, a tiny management services firm he runs, addressed to someone who left 18 months ago.

Mr Gunson told us he was currently working on a cutting reply.

AFTER lunch, we popped into see a friend at ChinTung International broking house, to ask his opinion about the disastrous land auction. He showed us a research document on the sale.

In the user column was one word: "God."

Was he trying to intimate that those secretive land agents at City Hall were investing in real estate for the Most Supreme Land Developer?

GOT to the office to find that David Gunson had composed a spoof Lunar New Year begging letter which he was going to send to McCann-Erickson in revenge.

It said: "We ourselves are planning a party soon, but it will be a grand affair and unfortunately we are short of readies to pay for the caviar. So we are contacting anybody who claims the SLIGHTEST connection with our esteemed firm to ask them to stump up. A contribution of HK$10,000 will keep one staff member happily in Beluga caviar for the duration, I can assure you."

We hope they will note the sarcasm.

You never know with advertising types.

SOMEONE from ChinTung rang. "'God' is shorthand for Godown," he said. Someone had better tell the Vicar of St John's.

JUST as we were thinking that we had not heard any Nasty Technology stories for a few days, what should happen but the Newsbyte correspondent in Hongkong bends our ear about a computer in Australia that told all members of the police force of New South Wales to go and book each other.

It started when a high ranking police officer failed to pay his parking ticket.

The Road and Traffic Authority computer put out the statutory number of warnings. When they were ignored, the computer automatically deregistered the car's owner — the New South Wales Police.

Every police car they had, marked and unmarked, became instantly illegal to drive and all police driving them became lawbreakers.

Police have been reluctant to name the high ranking officer involved. But we imagine he feels like pouring his coffee down the airvents of a certain machine.

READ something on the international news-wires that astounded us.

Businessmen give people headaches by their presence alone.

It is all to do with the striped shirts that are favoured by financial types, especially those of a conservative bent.

The stripes cause migraines and headaches, according to a study by a medical research council in Britain. In a number of cases the shirts are believed to be responsible for epileptic fits among colleagues.

Researchers say the wider the stripe and the brighter the colour, the more dangerous the shirt.

Have determined to meet Fast Buck (a bright wide stripe if ever we saw one) less frequently and use the phone more often.

UNFORTUNATELY, we had already booked dinner with Fast Buck at Gaddi's for tonight.

He had found new evidence for his theory that the June 4 "happening" had had a major under-the-surface effect on Hongkong.

He said the maternity ward at the Matilda Hospital was booked solid for March and there was a waiting list for expectant mums.

Other baby wards around Hongkong are also having an off-season boom.

Staff say that baby booms go in irregular waves, but March has not previously been known as a bulk delivery period, so to speak.

"Count back nine months and what do you get?" he asked.

"It appears that when the business prospects of Hongkong people were crumbling around their ears in June last year, large numbers took comfort in the, er, simple pleasures of life," he said.

He was wearing a striped shirt, so we attempted to keep our eyes averted.

AT the Peninsula that evening we heard The Tale of The Millionaires' Dentures.

One morning two American millionaires asked at reception for a boat so that they could go fishing in Hongkong waters.

A boat was duly arranged, and the two spent the day on the water.

One of them got seasick and discharged his expensive breakfast overboard − along with his dentures.

The other, who was not susceptible to seasickness, decided to play a joke on his friend. He took out his own false teeth, and hung them on the end of his fishing line.

Heaving the teeth out of the water, he said: "Look what I've just hooked."

"Grey! Dey muff be bine," mumbled his companion.

He unhooked the teeth and stuck them into his mouth.

But just as his friend was about to reveal the joke, the seasick gentleman realised the teeth did not fit him.

So he spat them back into the sea.

Yes, these are the sort of people who control the world's largest economy, on which Hongkong, an export-dependent place, totally relies to buy its products.

Wednesday
31
JANUARY

WOKE up with an awful headache from Fast Buck's striped shirt. Really must have a word with him about it.

DAVID Gunson called with some news. "The advertisers — God bless 'em — have taken the letter completely seriously," he said.

Mr Albert Yue of McCann-Erickson had written to him saying: "We note that you are having an office party and are short of funds to provide the necessary fare."

The bowtie-wearers had tracked down a pot of Beluga and delivered it to him — together with a bottle of champagne to wash it down.

The lawyer offered to share his winnings with us.

What a delightful outcome.

However, we made him promise not to tell the ICAC about this. To tell the truth, we were a bit nervous about the whole thing.

There are a lot of very large pot plants in the Prince's Building.

FIRST call of the morning was a summons from Dr Doom.

"I would like you to come and see me. Tomorrow. I have something MOST interesting to tell you," he said.

This gentleman, a tall, moustachioed Swiss stockbroker whose real name is Marc Faber, is often thought of as unorthodox.

We have no idea why. Just because he wears his hair long in a ponytail (despite being bald on top), rides a motorcycle, is an expert at the hula-hoop (he once took first prize in a competition), loves disco dancing, doubles as a Thai restaurateur, and always predicts precisely the opposite of what all the other stockbrokers forecast, there seems to be no reason to consider him odd.

The only thing strange is that he does not wear a dark suit. Sometimes he doesn't even wear a tie.

He believes that wearing a tie shortens a man's life by several years.

There are limits to unorthodoxy in the Hongkong business scene.

IN the bar during the evening, spotted Fast Buck. Made sure to keep our eyes averted from his shirt (thin blue pinstripes on white interlaced with a thicker pink line — DEFINITELY epilepsy-inducing).

But got close enough to hear the news that his company is to fly him to Bangkok for the weekend. All right for some.

Left hurriedly after feeling twinge of migraine.

HEARD from an unpatriotic American stockbroker:

The US Government is about to launch the new Vice-President Dan Quayle zero-coupon junk bond.

They have no principal, no interest and they never mature.

WHEN we entered his office, Dr Doom was leaning back from his desk in the New World Tower at a funny angle, his statue of Karl Marx appearing to read over his shoulder.

"Pardon me for not getting up to greet you," he said.

Then he pointed to the reason why: his foot, swathed in bandages, was on a stool at his side.

"Disco dancing," he said. "You know when you jump up and twirl about a bit and then come down?"

We confessed to being ignorant of that particular disco dancing movement, or indeed, any other.

"I came down on the wrong part of my foot and damaged it," he explained.

Dr Doom has acquired his nickname because he predicts catastrophe when other advisers are frothing with "sure winners".

This morning he did not disappoint.

"It's Japan. It is done for. The Nikkei Index is going to crash," he explained. "You had better print a warning in your column."

Consider yourselves warned.

POPPED into the FCC at lunch to find Luddite Lo in a feisty mood.

"Huh," he said. "Those people who think I am paranoid about this Easy Dialling Day disease had just jolly well better watch out, that's all. My cousin from Shanghai came to stay last night, and he tells me that THE SAME THING has happened there."

Some scheme is definitely afoot to telephonically isolate the major cities of the world, he said. He gave us a sheet of paper with the details, obtained by his cousin in Shanghai, to take back to the office to print in the newspaper.

AFTER reading them, we were aghast.

Never mind Easy Dialling Day. This operation in Shanghai, we can say without fear of contradiction, must be the most Mind-Bogglingly Mega-Complex Dialling Day ever.

From MBMCD Day, whenever it was, numbers being with a 2 had a 3 added before the 2. But numbers beginning with a 3 had a 4 added, and those beginning with a 4 had a 5 added. Numbers beginning with 5 had a 2 added in front, while 6 became 66. Numbers beginning with 70 became 470 while those beginning with 72 became 372, 79 became 379 and 84 became 884. There was more, but we couldn't keep up.

We will miss our friends in Shanghai.

DR Doom sent a fax. It explained that he was so sure of his predictions of doom for Japan, that he was telling all his clients to stake their cash on taking options or buying shorts on the Tokyo stock market.

The *Business Post* secretary asked why a grown-up stockbroker was buying shorts from Japan.

"They won't let him in the stock exchange wearing shorts," she said.

We patiently explained that buying "shorts" was a way of structuring your investment so that it goes up only if the share market comes down — a risky business. Buying "options" on shorts, like Dr Doom is doing, makes it a hundred times more profitable and an equal degree more risky, because it is leveraged, which means done with borrowed money.

But THESE are the sort of gambles Hongkong investors love — and they will try them more and more, if Fast Buck's money-mania theory is correct.

THAT evening, we met Lo in the jazz bar at trendy nitespot JJ's. He said he had been doing some more investigating.

"I am definitely onto something with this phone-number switching business," he hollared over the sound of the band.

"After Hongkong and Shanghai, it is about to hit London. London is going to have its own Easy Dialling Day disaster in less than three months."

He had been tipped off by a relative that British Telecom's Hongkong office had contacted Hongkong Telephone Co to find out how they did it. So that is goodbye London. This is serious business.

IT is hard to focus on things like hamburgers when major issues such as the collapse of the Japanese stock market and the Easy Dialling Day menace are imminent, but we forced ourselves.

This was because *Lai See's* first caller was the delightful Ms Angela Bassage, spokeswoman for McDonald's in Hongkong.

"We have had a very close call," she said. For several tense weeks it looked as if Hongkong was going to lose its crown as Fast Food Capital of the World.

"Because of the end of the Cold War," she explained dramatically.

Thousands of East Germans poured into Hungary on the way to West Germany in October and November last year. They stormed the counters of the Budapest branch of McDonald's to get a taste of the Western way of life — literally, she said. Sales broke all records.

The Hongkong staff were preparing to hand over their crown.

But Angela said the final count of sales worldwide had just been done. It showed a strong come-back from Hongkong fast-food fans in the second half. The final count revealed that the ravenous hordes in Sha Tin registered 2.59 million transactions last year.

This was a mere 20,000 more than the democracy-hungry East Germans produced in Budapest, but enough to keep Our Boys in first place.

Well done all concerned.

THAT evening, Fast Buck came straight to the FCC from the airport. He was wearing a flowered shirt, so we did not mind sitting next to him.

He had seen a thought-provoking scene in his

hotel in Bangkok. "This stern foreign businessman got to the counter to check out, and challenged many items on the bill — mini-bar, telephone calls and so on," he said. At the end there was an item which said: "Misc 600 baht."

The clerk smiled sweetly and said: "Oh, that is the charge for having an extra person in the room."

The businessman turned crimson, paid up without a murmur and left, said Buck.

"Clearly this hotel has found a way of making extra money from the little temptations that business men fall prey to in Bangkok," he added.

Interesting. Will expense account managers in Hongkong feel happy to pay bills for miscellaneous in Bangkok, however much she helps their executives relax, we wonder?

SEEN in a camping supplies shop by Tom Marrin of The Royal Trading Corp, Minden Avenue, Kowloon, was the following sign: "Now is the Winter we offer discount Tents."

Tuesday 6 FEBRUARY

"YOU idiot. Now you've published that stuff about hotel bills in Bangkok, all the company accountants in Hongkong will be backtracking through everyone's expense account records and noting who had 'Miscellaneous 600 baht' on their expense claims," thundered the anonymous voice on the phone at precisely 9 am.

Was that a twinge of guilt in his voice? Probably not.

INCIDENTALLY, woke up with a headache again. Must be Fast Buck's aftershave, not his striped shirts.

GOT back to the office to discover that Ms

Bassage had had discovered even more statistical confirmation of the importance of Hongkong consumers in the eyes of the McDonald's Corporation.

There are now 11,160 branches of McDonald's in the world.

When you grade them for numbers of transactions, guess how many of the top ten are in the United States?

Not one. How many of the top ten are in Hongkong? Five.

Our children are liable to grow up not knowing what a wonton is.

WEDNESDAY turned out rainy, so we took an early lunchbreak — otherwise it's impossible to get a taxi.

We were just about to consume the aforesaid lunch when a hand caught our elbow and made us lower the glass.

It was a stranger who wanted to talk about the Bangkok issue. "They are now charging for the presence of 'Ms Cellaneous' at virtually every hotel in Bangkok. But at the best hotels, they say: 'Excuse me sir, but would you like your guest to be put on a separate bill?'" he said.

Most business travellers would rather pay the guest bill themselves than risk having the company accountant ask for details of "miscellaneous".

We promised to pass this information on to readers through our column, although we were not free of qualms about the morality of doing so.

IN a surprise new policy, airports in Southeast Asia have started demanding that batteries be removed from electrical objects before passengers get on planes.

The chap who phoned up to tell us about it said he even had to take the tiny batteries out of his camera.

"I just thank God I don't have a pacemaker," he said.

NO signs of Dr Doom's warning coming true. The Japan market just seems to go up and up.

One company took out a large advertisement in the newspaper today to announce the launch of their new Japan Fund.

They reckon investors putting money into Japan are going to make it big.

WE now hear that Fast Buck is swanning off to Taipei on business for three days. So that is what a corporate financier does. What a life.

 Thursday
8
FEBRUARY

AT the office, found the desk buried with letters and faxes from business travellers to Bangkok showing bar bills that had caused them great embarrassment.

This stems from the modern habit of giving cocktails sexual names such as Orgasm.

"It is very hard to go to your company's financial director and ask to be reimbursed for the bill in your hand from a bar in Bangkok which says: 'Two Orgasms: 500 baht'," moaned one of the writers.

A CHAP called up in the afternoon and said he never drank alcohol, but still got into a mess with his company accountant.

"I had a Virgin Pina Colada, and they give me a bill which said:

'One Virgin — 200 baht.' I was teased for days by my colleagues after I got back to Hongkong. Except for one rather stingy chap, who asked me for the address."

"NO, no no. You've got it all wrong about Bangkok hotels," said the voice at the bar.

We are getting used to this by now.

Who did the speaker turn out to be but – actually we promised not to tell.

But tee hee. Fancy HIM getting up to that sort of thing! Difficult to imagine. The sheer poundage involved.

"The key is to always book a double room at the start," said the gentleman, who claimed to be experienced in these, er, affairs.

"This works out much cheaper than being made to pay the surcharge at the end."

The last time he checked in and asked for a double room, he said, the hotel clerk asked: "What is the name of your wife or girlfriend, sir?"

"I don't know," said the shameless businessman. "I haven't met her yet."

AH, the joys of the expat life. On a breezy late winter evening, we broke open a bottle of bubbly in the Royal Hongkong Jockey Club, and dissected the Last Days of Imperial Hongkong.

A banker told us about an ex-colleague of his, who, although ostensibly a foreigner, spoke perfect street-level Cantonese, complete with all the slang.

"It added a wonderful dimension to his life," he said. "After he collected his severance pay, he changed out of his pinstripes and like any true Hongkonger, went to the nearest Rolex shop."

The jeweller was very polite to his face, and then had a long discussion in Cantonese with his colleague about whether a customer this scruffy could possibly afford the watches he was asking to see.

"But an even more deflating put-down awaited him," said the banker. "He picked up a friend and went down to the massage parlour."

Once again, he was treated to the utmost degree of servility and politeness, this time from two girls who were about to, er, serve them.

Then one girl turned to the other and said in Cantonese: "Which one do you want? The fat one or the ugly one?"

Monday
12
FEBRUARY

IT'S the club mentality to blame for hangovers on Monday mornings, we are sure.

One cannot run out of signatures with which to pay bar bills.

Anyway, we got to work late this morning to find there had been several calls from Fast Buck who said he had had a lovely weekend in Taipei.

He told us his brief sojourn had dented his theory about the exodus-driven money-mania that is supposedly keeping the Hongkong economy ticking at high levels.

"If anything, the people of Taiwan are even more commercialised than the people of Hong-kong, and they don't have the spectre of 1997 hanging over them," he told us on the phone. "I'll have to re-think the theory a bit."

Arranged to meet at the bar tomorrow.

CALLED Five-Finger Wu to find him still on the hunt for the ideal export. He was checking out the products of Dah Wai Hongkong, a firm based in Queen's Road East.

Their flyers advertise interesting-sounding toilet tissues which are "warm-hearted". The price list includes a type of tissue called "New Three Pee". There are no indications as to what the name implies. Another charmingly named product is "Old People Diaper" at HK$80 for 30.

However, Chainsaw Charlie was not impressed. "Never sell in drugstores in the West with names like that. Tell him to try the joke shops."

Tuesday 13 FEBRUARY

BUCK'S most remarkable Taiwan tale was one about Mark Six, the Hongkong Government lottery.

Taipei is littered with commercialised altars, he said, where people will take your money and claim that the God of Mark Six will guide you to the right numbers.

"They even employ Taoist priests to give the whole thing an air of authenticity," he said.

They pray and chant all night just before the lottery is drawn, and you can see clouds of incense smog from the 1,200 commercialised altars in the city.

The authorities are just starting to crack down on it.

"They have given the assignment to the environmental protection department, because of all the smoke the operation produces," he said.

NIPPED into Five-Finger Wu's office in Causeway Bay to find him bouncing with excitement. He thinks he has finally found the substance that will make him rich: the cough mixture being sold by the Nin Jiom Medicine Manufactory in Texaco Road, Tsuen Wan.

He showed us the brochure. It prevents loss of voice "in people whose voice is their livelihood", gets rid of "pimples caused by lung infections", ensures the benefits of an undisturbed night's sleep, gets rid of colds quickly, fixes dryness of the skin, cures bad breath, and counteracts the effects of smoking and drinking.

All this from a cough mixture.

"Heaven knows what the Nin Jiom Medicine Manufactory will produce when they become a bit more ambitious," said Wu.

SAW Dr Doom at California restaurant in Lan Kwai Fong in the evening.

Since his predication about Tokyo collapsing, the share market in that country has done almost nothing but move in the opposite direction.

Strange. He is still so sure that disaster is approaching that he seemed positively elated, despite being prevented from indulging in the excesses of breakdancing because of his foot.

Wednesday 14 FEBRUARY

MARKETING people in Hongkong are the best in the world.

They are doing an amazing direct mail job within the Royal Hongkong Police Force, according to a shiny-domed policeman we had a chat with in the afternoon.

The product being touted is a remedy for baldness called Zhang Fa Bao, marketed by Coxston. (We have notified Five-Finger Wu, in case this is the potion that will make his fortune.)

Nostalgic domeheads rub the goo on those barren acres, and thick layers of bushy undergrowth soon appear, according to the brochure.

First coup: the company has got hold of a list of members of Asia's Finest, complete with identification numbers and police force internal phone numbers.

Second coup: the marketing people know who is bald and who isn't, since only dazzle-headed officers have received them.

We put in a call to police HQ for an official comment.

None received at the time we sneaked out of the office.

A BAFFLED policeman called back this morning and told us that as far as he knew, there was no central document at police headquarters listing offices by proportion of denuded scalp.

But as Luddite Lo would say, you never know what information about you is filed away on a computer somewhere.

WE were spending a pleasant hour in a traffic jam at the Cross-Harbour Tunnel in Causeway Bay when we noticed something.

You know the giant Shell cards that balance on top of Shell petrol stations in Hongkong?

They have no expired. They are all three months out of date.

What a go-ahead impression of the Shell company that leaves us with.

BACK in the office after a pleasant lunch at the Sheraton, we had a call from Mr Mike Yalden, who works in the far reaches of Tai Po.

He told us he had asked one of his staff to trek to Tsim Sha Tsui to the Trade Department to pick up a Certificate of Origin for the engineering products he handles. For this, the underling had to have stamps totalling HK$75 on the form.

This peon went up to the counter with his form, duly bearing three HK$20 stamps and three HK$5 stamps.

"But the application was refused, because they were the WRONG COMBINATION of stamps," alleged an astounded-sounding Mr Yalden.

Staff explained that the HK$75 had to be in a combination of one HK$50 stamp, one HK$20 stamp, and one HK$5 stamp.

We are in a state of frank disbelief. This is *laissez-faire* Hongkong. Asked a colleague to slip into the Trade Department on his way home to see if this is true.

Friday 16 FEBRUARY

OUR colleague told us' that it was entirely accurate. The Trade Dept only accepts one combination of stamps for each form.

We called Mike Yalden and suggested that the next time the Trade Department wrote to him, he reject the letter saying that he only accepted letters in mauve polka-dotted envelopes stuck down with a particular brand of glue.

That's the only sort of reaction they will understand.

THERE are strange rumours going about that Drexel Burnham Lambert in the United States is about to go bankrupt. This is the parent company of Dr Doom's firm.

We wonder if he can arrange options to sell short his own company?

Saturday 17 FEBRUARY

ON an afternoon stroll through Central, we bumped into Polytechnic librarian Roy Stall, who showed us a menu from the Village Restaurant at Stanley Main Street.

For HK$36 the restaurant will serve you "Indonesian Nazi Goreng".

"NAZI Goreng? Served in Stanley? Does the military know about this?" he asked. "Maybe it should read Nazi Goering?"

WE were just having a quick tea-time snack (no, it was not a Big Mac, but came in a tumbler with soda water) when we got a call from Ms Jane Ram, who has just received a fresh communication from the computer which is apparently in love with her at the bank.

"The statement is much the same as the others – except it says: 'MAKE USE OF YOUR CARD,'" she said.

"I think it's teasing me."

HAD a call from our Cathay Pacific Airways mole.

He said he was going to send us a secret internal report he had smuggled out.

We rubbed our hands with glee.

STILL no sign of the Japan market crashing. In fact, one finance firm today announced the creation of a Japan Warrant Fund, which will amplify the movement of the Japanese market for investors.

All the movement, of course, being in an upward direction.

Dr Doom's investors must be getting impatient.

"SO even the rats are leaving Hongkong," said Chainsaw Charlie, chewing on a piece of metal that had fallen out of the back of his Atex computer. "Talk about an ominous sign for people on a sinking ship."

The secret report from Cathay Pacific had arrived first thing in the morning via a no-return-number fax.

Called *The Hunt for Grey January,* it described an airline passenger, genus *ratus ratus,* who took a flight on a Cathay Pacific jet on January 18 between Hongkong and Singapore.

It was spotted coming out of first class, where it had decided to take a peek at Marco Polo business class before heading off the food carts to see what was for lunch.

Flight engineer GB Sperring lunged for the rat. "I attempted to catch it when it appeared, but as I did, one of our girls spotted it — and grabbed hold of me," he wrote.

They eventually did catch it. The flight engineer warned in the report that hungry rats had in the past been known to eat through electrical cables on planes.

Actually, we thought the food in the Marco Polo section of Cathay flights was quite adequate.

The metaphysical significance of a rat leaving Hongkong in business class was not lost on us.

AHA. A message from the Trade Department's Mrs Regina Ip, concerning the choice of stamps on application forms.

"We have instructed our counter staff not to reject similar applications but to refer them to their supervisors for interpretation."

In some distant forest, we have saved several trees.

OH dear. We hear that Drexel Burnham Lambert in America is about to go completely bankrupt.

How unfortunate for all concerned.

Dr Doom must be an unhappy man.

THE day started with a call from a mysterious voice on the phone.

He asked us to pass on this message to readers:

We must all keep an eye out for American business people in Hongkong pretending they cannot speak English; trying to get through immigration by flashing their bank cards; attempting to get into hotel rooms booked in other people's names; and fleeing from the scenes of accidents.

What should you do if you see the above?

"Smile. Go and shake the person's hand. He is a terrified business traveller primed for international jet—setting," said the voice.

Business travellers from the United States are now studying the *Travel Security Guide,* prepared by financial services firm American International Group.

The voice, a shy man from the insurance industry, told us that he was going to send us a copy.

THE Texas Chainsaw Sub-Editor had a suggestion about what should be done about the bankruptcy of Dr Doom's parent firm, Drexel Burnham Lambert.

"They should arrange to be rescued by Merrill Lynch. Then we would have a new firm called Lynch and Burnham. Har har har."

He is not a sentimental man.

THE guide for American business travellers arrived in the mail this morning. Here are extracts:

If your own name is easily recognised, have an associate make your reservations in his or her name.

On a foreign airline, avoid speaking English as much as possible.

Select your own taxi, avoiding the first and second in the line.

If you witness or are involved in a traffic accident, do not stop — the accident may be contrived. Instead, proceed to your destination and report the accident to the host group and police.

Avoid wearing singularly "American" fashions such as "plaid trousers for men" and "tourist indicators" such as cameras (we thought Americans only dressed like that in European films).

If asked to produce identification, avoid using your passport. Show something like a bank card instead.

People in Hongkong who run clinics for the unbalanced had better prepare for an influx of referrals.

THE only cheering thing this week was a speech from Hongkong's Banking Commissioner, Mr Tony Nicolle.

He said that even if all the forex dealers flew off to Hongcouver, er, Vancouver, there would still be enough business to go around, because the Hongkong economy was buzzing along at a good rate.

He was clearly trying to defuse worries about 1997, about the June 4 "occurrence" and the emigration rush and so on.

"It is fashionable these days to colour any assessment of Hongkong with pessimism. These Jonahs serve us ill," said Mr Tony Nicolle.

THE *South China Morning Post* librarian was amazed when we asked for a Bible.

"For the business desk?" she asked, her eyebrows meeting her hairline.

The Bible confirmed what we suspected. The Banking Commissioner has got his prophets mixed up. It was Jeremiah who was the Prophet of Doom. Jonah was the one who was told to preach destruction but didn't want to and ran away instead.

Chainsaw Charlie pointed out that Jonah then ended up being swallowed by a whale. "And that's how most people in Hongkong feel about their futures anyway," he said, cynically.

THERE was a financial newsletter from Dr Doom in the *Lai See* pigeon-hole today.

The collapse of parent firm Drexel Burnham Lambert was "a symptom of debt liquidation leading to lower share prices" — something he had predicted.

The end of Drexel has proved him right and put him out of a job.

"The next market letter will be published from an all-night taxi company's dormitory or a farm in Thailand," he wrote.

MET the Lamma Looker for lunch at the Cafe de Paris on Lan Kwai Fong.

He was amused by the idea that American business travellers should not take the first or second taxis available, especially in a city known for the rudeness of taxi-drivers.

"Here in Hongkong, the taxi drivers arrange that for you," he said.

GOT another call from the Lamma Looker, who told us that on the way to work, he spotted 29 trams in a row in Johnston Road, Wan Chai. "Is this a record?" he asked.

"No," we replied. "It must be Hongkong Tramways putting together a system to help nervous American business travellers."

GOOD Lord. Got to the office to find complete

and utter chaos at the business desk. The Tokyo Stock Market has completely collapsed.

Phones were ringing, reporters were scurrying in and out, and the artists were frantically sketching graphs.

So Dr Doom was right all along. He must be a happy man, not to mention a rich one. Must remember to ring him tomorrow and congratulate him.

JAPAN market still tumbling. Finally got through to Dr Doom to congratulate him on the profits his Japanese "shorts" must be bringing him.

He wasn't celebrating. Because of the collapse of Drexel Burnham Lambert, Dr Doom has been forced to cover his "shorts" on Nikkei Index futures.

He had to close all the commodity positions and transfer the funds into insured securities accounts.

How unfair life is. But the good Doctor was reasonably sanguine.

He still has a few private little "shorts" on Japanese shares.

"So I can still enjoy the carnage a bit," he said. But he sounded like he was putting on a brave face.

SO there we were, sitting on the Star Ferry, second class, behind three visiting American tourists. One of them was sorting though a wad of local banknotes, trying to make some sense of the bewildering variety of colours, issuing banks and vintages.

The Chinese junk of the Hongkong Bank HK$10 was easily identified, as was the rival banks' headquarters.

The Tiger Balm pagoda on the Hongkong Bank HK$100 was trickier, but one of the tourists remembered it from the a coach tour the previous day.

It was the Hongkong Bank HK$50 that had them all stumped. Then one of them had a brainwave.

"Got it!" he said. "It's a junk-full of Vietnamese refugees coming into the harbour."

Has anyone else noticed that nobody outside Hongkong has the SLIGHTEST understanding about major issues within the territory?

GOT out our credit card to pay for lunch at Dan Ryan's in Pacific Place.

"Don't you have cash?" asked our companion, that trading company employee and well-known techno-phobe Mr Luddite Lo (who has taken to wearing circular Canto-pop sunglasses everywhere, including indoors and in the cinema).

He told us that he had given up using plastic money, because it leaves a record of everything you buy.

"Nice, comfortable, untraceable cash is much more in the Hongkong style," he said.

If the cashless society is on its way, it's going

to have trouble absorbing him.

The upshot of all this was that HE had to pay for our rather boozy lunch, so we did not complain too much. His phobia may well prove expensive to maintain.

STUMBLED back to the office at three-ish.

While performing a natural function in the men's room at our luxurious offices, we seemed to hear melodious warbling voices floating through the air.

Perhaps we should take more solids with our lunch? Hic.

Friday 2 MARCH

HAD a visit from the young lady who toils in the office opposite us in the Taikoo Trading Estate for American Express.

We mentioned our friend's objections about plastic money, and she fought back with news of an incident which reaffirmed her belief that plastic money was the future.

A recent American Airlines flight to England was diverted to Scotland because of fog. The pilot was rather worried about this, since American Airlines had no contract with any fuel companies in the vicinity.

But someone told him that Esso Aviation had signed up as an American Express merchandiser last year.

So he taxied his plane to the nearest Esso station and flashed his American Express Card.

"I never leave home without it," he said.

"That'll do nicely, sir," said the fuel pump man. The plane swallowed 9,000 gallons of fuel.

We only hope his Amex bill wasn't paid from his personal account by autopay.

What would Luddite Lo have done in that situation? We don't know, but he DOES carry a lot of cash.

TODAY we also learnt the source of the warbling sounds audible in the *South China Morning Post* toilets when the wind blows west.

American Express has invested in a karaoke machine and lounge for its staff.

If they get weary of adding up the purchases on your statement, they simply saunter off to the karaoke room, belt out a couple of verses of *Life is a Cabaret Old Chum* and then get back to work.

The firm has now added the karaoke machine as a "perk" on its recruitment advertising.

At least we know WE will never work there. Wouldn't pass the audition.

Saturday 3 MARCH

FELT like a bit of a binge this weekend, so went out to the Wine Cellar in Prince's Building with Chainsaw Charlie.

Chainsaw is a bit of a connoisseur when it comes to fine wines. He buried himself in a list of imported wines from Chile and chose the Sauvignon Blanc Semillon 1988.

This had an amazing note under the listing which said: "Plenty of fruit and flowers on the nose."

"That's what you are supposed to wear when you drink it," we said with a straight face. "It's a Chilean custom."

"Really?" he said.

"No." He didn't laugh. Why must wine-snobs take their boozing so seriously?

Monday 5 MARCH

JUNK skipper yesterday was strictly instructed to avoid sewage outlets and floating garbage platforms. So he settled the junk in an area of water off the coast of Sai Kung, which he described as "nice pink colour, pretty-pretty".

SKIN felt distinctly tingly as we arrived at work on Monday morning.

No time to worry about it. Even before we opened the mail, there was an annoyingly bright voice on the phone.

"I read that you were thinking about getting a job with American Express, but felt you weren't a good enough singer. Don't fret, take a Macintosh computer with you," said the caller, a computer buff.

He described a new device called Farallon's MacRecorder 2.0 which enables even someone as gravel-voiced as us to join American Express without fear of being embarrassed at the interview, even if it is all done in song.

It enables your computer to memorise your voice and sing or speak in it.

IN the mail was a chain letter which said: "Kiss someone you love when you get this letter."

It seems to us that the *Business Post* secretary always runs off to hide in the toilets after she delivers one of these to our desk.

But perhaps she is just enjoying the singing of the Amex staff.

FIRST thing in the morning, the computer buff called again.

He had made a new discovery with his machine.

You could use the voice-processing machine to alter the speed of the playback without changing the pitch. Replay at high speed and you sound normal, not like Mickey Mouse.

"Or you could secretly record your boss's

voice and slow down his or her voice without distortion, which makes them sound heavily tranquilised, on drugs or dangerously deranged," he said.

Would love to try it on a certain headline writer in our office, but don't think anyone would notice a difference.

ENVIRONMENT correspondent told us about the Red Tide problems in the waters around Hongkong. Skin breaking into mosaic patterns.

WE got another "kiss someone" chain letter this morning. We could tell because the secretary rushed off to hide in the toilet again.

But this one was particularly worrying. It was in a Dataquest envelope and had a computer-printed address.

Since Dataquest is a market research firm, it must have a huge bank of Hongkong addresses. It is frightening to think what could happen if a chain letter nut started using high tech mailing equipment.

We called Dataquest managing director Joseph Lung to ask if he knew about it. He didn't, and from the tone of his voice he hopes to find out who is doing it.

And when he does, we don't think he is planning to kiss them.

FOR someone who claims to be the ultimate techno-phobe, Luddite Lo spends an awful long time on the phone.

He was on again this morning, talking about an article in the newspaper about a Californian company launching a micro-chip identification system for pets.

You pay them US$40 and a veterinarian implants a tiny electronic chip under the loose skin between the shoulders of the pet.

"What's so threatening about that?" we asked Lo. "It's only for cats and dogs, isn't it?"

"So far," he said. "But now they have the technology . . . I don't know about you but I'm going to make sure my boss doesn't see any copies of today's newspaper."

Friday 9 MARCH

IN the walkway outside the new Hang Seng Bank headquarters building in Central we saw a sign saying: "Watching your step."

Who is watching our step? And what happens if we step out of line?

BACK in the office, we found a fax from our teacher friend Ms Pedant.

"We all make spelling missteaks," she wrote.

Which is why she was inclined to shrug off a promotional sheet by the Gestetner office people which twice spelt commercial as "commerical" and spelt process as "processe". It almost became too much to ignore after she noticed the page was about "thorough inspection procedures".

And then she noticed another word spelt wrongly twice on the page. "Please note, Gestetner copywriters, your own name is spelt Gestetner. Not Gestenter," she said.

Saturday 10 MARCH

A BOTTLE of Chivas Regal arrived on our desk yesterday morning.

Attached was a compliments slip from Jack Crook, boss of Gestetner International.

"Congratulations," said a note. "This is first prize for spotting our deliberate mistakes."

Have sent the bottle to Ms Pedant, ICAC please note.

Sunday 11 MARCH

"IF Hongkong people are driven by this money-mania to make money to get out of here, then why do people waste such huge amounts of money at Happy Valley and Sha Tin race-courses?"

The speaker was Ms Pedant, with whom we were brunching at the FCC.

We replied with the now famous tale of how an old woman put down a stake of HK$10 on the horses at Happy Valley, went off to do some shopping, and then returned to pick up HK$40 million in winnings.

How did she do it? It was said to be a double trio, which is a bet in which you nominate the first three horses in two consecutive races.

Monday 12 MARCH

THE stock market of Hongkong is still in the doldrums.

Chainsaw Charlie, who put his annual bonus into Hongkong Bank shares, was feeling morose.

"Mood worsens. Markets fall. While I am feeling pessimistic, here's a pessimism joke," he said.

"How many pessimists does it take to change a light bulb?

"None. After all, what's the point? It's just going to burn out again, anyway." One can gauge his confidence level pretty well by that.

MS Pedant called to say she had had a brilliant idea. She suggested that she and ourselves form a joint venture offering a spelling tuition service for Hongkong companies.

"Good idea," we said. "We could call it Kwik-Spel."

She did not think this was a suitable name.

SOMEONE, somewhere, is putting out a publication for every interest.

Just arrived on the shelves is a book called *How to Shit in the Woods: An Environmentally Sound Approach to a Lost Art.*

That's right, "Art".

US-based author Kathleen Meyer says she wrote it "after years of practical experience".

We have sent off for a copy.

Perhaps she will visit Hongkong on a launch tour?

We thought about inviting her round to the office for an interview but Chainsaw Charlie, who is rather office-proud about our department, vetoed the idea.

THE local junk mail people have finally gone stark raving mad.

Hongkong music industry man Andreas Panayi telephoned to tell us that his CAR had received advertising material.

This was your usual subscribe-now-and-save-money letter, inviting it to order *Time* magazine, he said.

"It's a good car," he said. "But it can't read."

The letter was not addressed to him, but to his vehicle, neatly identified at the right address by its registration number.

We called *Time* magazine, who said they had not yet descended to the point of sending junk mail to inanimate objects, with the possible exception of Hongkong senior civil servants.

They promised to sort through their voluminous records to find out how it happened.

TIME magazine called later with the results of their detective work: the magazine's subscription computer had done a one-for-one address swap with Swedish Motors customer listing computer.

Copies of *Time* magazine in Hongkong will shortly get invitations to test drive Saabs.

Friday 16 MARCH

TRADER Trevor Hughes of Gerard Commodities phoned to say he had come across a product in which we might be interested for our offbeat collection: Universal Stinking Smell Dispelling Detergent.

The publicity material starts: "In our life, nobody doesn't dislike stinking smell."

(We're still trying to work that one out.)

"Not only does it trouble one's studies, but also makes one loath for food. What is more, it makes one throw up, damages one's digestion and nerves and endangers one's health. It is nothing short of human's arch enemy."

The makers, Guangzhou Yixiang Chemical Enterprises of Luhu Road, Guangzhou, recommend it for use in slaughter houses, surgical theatres and sewage treatment plants.

"Free from harm and any side effects, our product, safe and easy to use, can in fact promote the growth of crops. Indeed, Universal Brand Stinking Smell Dispelling Detergent is your very good friend in life."

It sounds a fine product, despite the fact that there is no tradition of crop-growing in surgical theatres in Hongkong or the West.

But it needs a snappier name. UniStink? StinkOut? PongOff? WhiffStop?

Monday 19 MARCH

DIDN'T go to the office this morning. Why waste working hours trekking down to Quarry Bay? Instead, went straight to lunch at Brown's in Exchange Square.

There we heard that the ghost of the Duke of Connaught had returned. And he is NOT in a good mood.

Inmates of Jardine House told us that there has been a definite increase in inexplicable problems at the building, ever since the name was changed from Connaught Centre to Jardine House.

Electrical things have been going wrong, and there has been sporadic bursting of air-conditioning pipes.

A legal firm in the building was almost flooded when water started pouring into offices.

Tuesday 20 MARCH

THE bigger the press release, the smaller the news — that's a classic newspaper maxim, that we have just made up.

An example is the announcement received today that an "intelligent buildings conference" is to be held in summer.

This conjures up visions of the Hongkong Bank headquarters sitting around swapping chit-chat with the Exchange Square triplets: "My underfloor wiring's really neat but I get the occasional draught up my atrium."

Congratulations to Asia Pacific Exhibitions of Singapore for the remarkable feat of sending out 13 pages of press releases on intelligent buildings without once even attempting to define what they are.

A HELPFUL architect called to explain that in the simplest terms, intelligent buildings are places in which the electrical and mechanical system is deeply integrated with computers.

"They are buzzing with technological possibilities, sometimes literally," he said.

Happened to have lunch booked with Luddite Lo at Grissini's in the Grand Hyatt. Showed him the press releases, and, as one can imagine, he was not very keen on the idea of bringing buildings to life.

He read the material with growing horror — especially the bit that said that at the confab in Singapore on July 12 and 13, Ian Flood will talk on 'Solving Constructional Operational Problems Using Artificial Neural Networks and Simulated Evolution.'

"Let them start evolving, and who knows what we'll end up with," warned Lo.

MORE strange goings-on at Jardine House.

This afternoon, one of the glass doors suddenly shattered, spraying itself all over the steps.

"There was no one even standing near it. It just shattered into tiny pieces, like sugar," we were told by a mystified eye witness who subscribes to the angry ghost theory.

WE hear that at this brainy buildings show there will even be something for people who live in stupid buildings.

"Retrofitting" is what they call making them intelligent. Curious that they have not invented the same technique for people.

A firm called OKI will be talking about their system which enables the building to "identify and locate" the persons inside it.

This fills us with dread. Picture yourself washing your hands in the smallest room (listening to the American Express accountant singing *Credit Where Credit's Due*) when the plumbing suddenly says: "You've been here ten minutes. Get back to your desk."

IN the afternoon, gadgaholic Matthew Crampton popped in to tell us not to be so technophobic: technology could be a wonderful thing.

He showed us a dynamite alarm clock, made by Team Concepts Electronics of Pak Hong Tin Street, Sha Tin.

This shouts a ten-second warning before starting a countdown. If you fail to shut it off in time there is an enormous explosion.

Have a heart attack at 7 am. What a way to start the day.

TODAY we got yet another press release about buildings. Up and coming is the Fourth World

Conference of Tall Buildings in the Urban Habitat. The local organiser is the Hongkong Institution of Engineers.

Will nobody stand up for short stupid buildings like ours?

Monday 26 MARCH

DECIDED to cut down all the needless travel even further. Went straight to the FCC for our evening appointment, and decided to keep in touch with the office and Brown's from the phone next to the bar.

Also waiting for the bar to open was Nigel Simmonds of *The Peak* magazine. He handed us a business card which describes him as a "Feather Writer".

Does this mean he is concentrating entirely on lightweight matters?

Or has Cheney Communications decided to build up a team of specialised writers focusing on highly specific fashion topics? Will there also be a sequin writer and a fish leather writer?

"I like to think that this refers to the standard of writing technology at Cheney Communications rather than the weight of my writing," said Mr Simmonds, who has received a bulk delivery of four boxes of the misprinted business cards.

HIS story reminded us of the medical man from the navy who was asked his profession. He replied: "I'm a naval doctor."

"Amazing," came the reply. "I didn't know doctors specialised to such an extent."

Wednesday 28 MARCH

MET another inmate from *The Peak* magazine at the bar. Jill Entwistle's business cards describe her as "Dupty Editor".

Got back to the office to find that the *Peak's* publisher, Christopher Cheney, had faxed us a letter.

"I must take exception to references to low levels of technology within Cheney Communications," said Mr Cheney. "The editorial department has a typewriter. And once we train staff to stop dropping food into it, we will probably buy them an electric one."

He signs himself "Choirman".

THE German Business Association lunch to be held at the Regal Meridien Hotel tomorrow will feature Mr Walter Sulke, OBE, JP, chairman of Zung Fu, the company that keeps Hongkong up to its chin in Mercedes Benz cars.

He will deliver a speech entitled "Why Are We Still Here?"

This is fascinating.

Particularly since Zung Fu announced last week that it was relocating its head office to Bermuda, because of 1997 fears.

OUR copy of *How to Shit in the Woods* arrived.

It is in two parts: how to discharge your, er, duties in dignity and comfort, and how to do it with environmental awareness.

It covers fine points such as basic squatting positions, getting above the high water lines so as not to cause pollution, and digging a hole.

Fascinating reading, but we don't think it will be a big-seller in Hongkong.

Local people would fall at the first hurdle: first, find your woods.

A LOCAL caller told us he had had an unusual experience with misprinted business cards in Hongkong.

He once ordered a set with his title "Psychotherapist" on them.

When they arrived, his broadminded Hongkong printer had written "Psycho The Rapist."

Not the sort of thing to put his patients at their ease.

But a good example of how Hongkong service industries will perform any service for anyone, without asking any indiscreet questions.

AFTER a pleasant slumber at the FCC bar over a Sunday brunchtime, we picked up the bill to see that we had apparently consumed more than 280 glasses of dry sherry. This added up to well over $1,000.

We don't even LIKE sherry. A quick analysis of the number and type of empty vessels upon our sq. m. of bar surface confirmed our opinion that the bill was wrong.

The barman, fortunately, did not dispute this fact.

"New computer system. Not used to it yet,"

he said, taking back the bill.

We hope they don't make the same mistake with Chainsaw Charlie, who probably wouldn't spot the error.

TO calm ourselves, we settled in a comfortable chair to read the latest *Peak* magazine.

This featured a shocking story about government plans to BAN mobile telephones in Hongkong because of a recent "destabilising incident".

At a pro-democracy rally in Happy Valley, wrote Nigel Simmonds, Legislative Councillor Martin Lee apparently started CONDONING the Tiananmen Square crackdown over the PA system, speaking in Mandarin.

How could this be?

In fact, the message coming out over the PA system turned out to be interference from a portable telephone being used in the nearby New China News Agency headquarters.

The crowd were infuriated.

Eventually, Mr Lee explained that he had been temporarily possessed by a demon spirit.

Shocking stuff, indeed. But banning mobile phones completely seems a bit over the top.

Monday 2 APRIL

LATE to work this morning, and had to dash off almost immediately to lunch.

At the FCC, made the embarrassing discovery that large flakes of gold, well okay, gold paint, were flaking off our fake Rolex, bought at great expense (HK$225) at the Temple Street Night Market.

This was unhelpfully pointed out in a highly public place, the main bar, by Chainsaw Charlie, who revels in tactlessness.

We loudly expounded a theory about the effect of Hongkong humidity on the best quality gold, but don't think we were believed.

Honestly, you can't even get decent quality fakes these days. What is Hongkong coming to?

"TAIWAN," whispered the caller furtively. "That's the place to buy them. The quality is much better than elsewhere. They spend more time on them, and are more careful doing the faces, so the results are better. They also put weights in the watches. If you pick up a Bangkok Rolex, you can tell it is fake because it is so light. The Taiwanese ones feel right. Some of them are actually gold-plated, which means that they don't turn a funny colour after a few months."

Gold-plated Taiwanese Rolexes, the mysterious voice told us, cost US$45.

SURPRISED to get a call on the subject of counterfeit watches from Hongkong City Polytechnic lecturer Robin Bradbeer.

"I have been reading your items about fake watches. I must admit I have an interest in fakes — academic only," he said.

The prof said he had made a study of fakes in the region and yesterday's mystery caller was right: Taiwan was definitely producing the best ones.

Like the real thing, their movements are mechanical, which means the second hand sweeps smoothly around the face. Traditional fakes have quartz innards, so their second hands travel in short sharp movements.

"The parts that cannot be made are genuine Rolex spares, or so the makers claim," he said.

MET Robin Bradbeer for lunch at the Hyatt Regency.

"There is a new craze among buyers of fake watches in Hongkong," he said. "You buy a fake Rolex but get a real strap to go with it. Real Rolex straps are available in Temple Street, Mongkok for about HK$1,500, which make the HK$200 fakes look much more real."

Suddenly realised, to our extreme horror, that we were having this conversation next to a large and bushy ficus religiosa.

If this conversation gets back to the ICAC by any means, we would just like them to know that this information is for reference only.

THERE was a late-night knock on the door at "Lai See Mansions" in Causeway Bay.

Our neighbour, marketing man Baden Gilmore, said he wanted to show us his underpants.

He wasn't drunk. He just wanted to expound his theory that there was some confusion in the counterfeiting industry's underpants division.

"You know how men's undies in the West are always marketed with macho brand names such as HOM or Eminent?" he said.

Well the brand now selling like hot cakes in the Temple Street Night Market in Yau Ma Tei is called "Him's".

Baden showed us a pack, on which was written: "This trunk top elastic with the word HIM's woven in, please remember this name."

But this is the bizarre bit. Open the packet and what do you find? A pair of apparently genuine

Calvin Klein designer underpants with the familiar mauve-gray insignia embroidered along the top.

"Have the copycats moved from selling fake goods in famous name packaging to selling real goods in fake packages?" he asked.

HAD a call from a sniggering Nigel Simmonds today.

His story about mobile telephones being banned in Hongkong was an April Fool's joke.

All the worried people who called Mr Simmonds in the past few days, including officials from CSL and Hongkong Telecom, can breathe easy.

It was obvious, actually, but we didn't want to spoil his joke.

DRINK yourself skinny! Oh, yes, yes, yes.

This is the product Five-Finger Wu has been waiting for for years. We shall leave some on Chainsaw's desk.

Fat Reduction Tea is made by Lam's Trading Co of Pei Ho Street, Sham Shui Po.

We discovered it after an afternoon's snooping around the old-fashioned medical shops of Western district, which specialise in deer testicles, etc.

The box says:

"This product has remarkable effect in promoting metabolism and excretion of adipose." Adipose is the scientific name for fat.

"Moreover, the users will continue to have good appetite after taking it, so can enjoy delicious food as usual."

A drink that makes you excrete your fat must be worthwhile, although it sounds *extremely* painful.

A RIVAL slimming tea is on the market, we learned today at the FCC. It is called Chinese Kipling Keepfit Tea.

Tea enthusiast Gilly Beal of Media Dynamics showed us a pack she had got from M&A Co of Causeway Bay. The packet says it "resolves" bodily fat, whatever that means, and you don't even need to eat less. "No diet needed."

The most intriguing claim: "It also rids you of bad breath and erosion of the lip and tongue."

This is a new one on Gilly. "I had never thought about the dangers of lip or tongue erosion, or indeed, of other bodily parts," she said.

"Perhaps that's what happens if you drink too much of the tea that we wrote about yesterday, the one that makes you excrete your fat?" we suggested.

THIS business about finding the most remarkable piece of Chinese medicine is fast becoming a contest.

Five-Finger Wu today came up with a virility and longevity drug which is advertised as being used by China's senior leaders, and must explain why they live so long.

Chinese Wonderful Prescription (CWP), distributed by Washer International Co, comes in pills (24 for HK$500) or suppositories (12 for HK$500).

"The average life span of those family members who insist on taking CWP is 91 years," according to documents from the firm.

It allegedly has an amazing effect on the

sexual functions of men. The company knows this because they fed some to a hamster and its testicles put on weight, though heaven only knows how they detected this.

In an accompanying testimonial, a chap called Zhou, aged 44, writes: "Owing to swimming to cause my loins and legs to be pain by the frigid, I had no sexual desire about the recent half year due to sexual function going down. After taking CWP I can have sexual intercourse three days later. CWP is wonderful."

A man of great patience.

HAD nightmares about trying to insert a two-inch suppository into a five-inch hamster.

GOT to work bleary-eyed to find a reader had sent in a packet of Yuwang Weight Reducing Bath Foam, made by Yuwang Corp of Beijing.

This works with "mysterious efficiency on bathing, weight reducing, skin protection and health caring".

While cleansing your skin, the bath foam "promotes the metabolism of local fat on legs, hips etc, so as to meet the aim of reducing weight and becoming healthy and beautiful-looking".

This sounded worth writing about.

We asked the Texas Chainsaw Sub-Editor whether he thought it was really possible to have a bath additive in which you could sit for 10 to 20 minutes and then lose weight.

"Sure," he said. "You could do it with any form of extra-corrosive acid."

SATURDAY dawned bright and unusually

humid, and, just for a change, we decided to take lunch at the Luk Yu Tea House on Stanley Street.

There we bumped into journalist Eric Stone of *Asian Business* magazine, clutching a large package, which he said he would unveil to us if he could find a dark enough corner.

It turned out to be a plastic object with a nozzle. He put his lips to it and said: "Don't (puff) assume that the only things (puff) they are churning out of factories in China (puff) are boring bicycles and tractors (puff)."

The floppy plastic object soon revealed itself to be an inflatable plastic sheep. It is called The Love Ewe, costs US$14.95 and is inflatable up to the approximate dimensions of a medium-sized dog.

The packaging says: "Better than the real thing. No annoying bleating."

This item is being exported in large numbers to San Francisco, and frankly, we are not surprised.

Monday 16 APRIL

NOT much doing, news-wise today. The only intriguing call was from Hongkong computer disk exporter Mike Lovett of Bonaseal Co.

He said he had sent a telex about a business deal to Nwo-Son and Co of Lagos five weeks ago.

For more than a month, he heard nothing. Then yesterday he got a reply.

"I'm going to send you a copy," he said.

Tuesday 17 APRIL

THE letter to Mike Lovett was on our desk when we arrived in the morning.

"Urgency-Urgency-Urgency," it said across

the top. Mr Harrison Harmann of Nwo-Son writes:

"Sorry for our late reply due to we were on burial ceremony for our 'AREA CHAIRMAN' who died of brief illness on 21/2/90 which prompted us to have a short break for '3 weeks' in memorial for him."

Now you can't feel angry with staff who are so soft-hearted that they spend three weeks mourning when their area chairman dies, now can you?

The firm's marketing manager Mr Kalu Nwojo is to visit Hongkong to sign the export contract.

"He will stay with you five weeks," says the letter.

"Like hell he will," said Mr Lovett.

Nwo-Son Co has a curious idea about the time things take.

Wednesday 18 APRIL

IT'S update time for trendy speakers. We hear on excellent authority (the people next to us at California bar yesterday evening) that it is no longer acceptable, even for male chauvinists, to say: "I'll get my girl to call your girl and we'll do lunch."

The new "in" phrase is: "Speak to my Breadhead".

We don't think the Business Post secretary is going to like it.

Thursday 19 APRIL

NO, a Breadhead is not a secretary. "Speak to my Breadhead" is actually a revival of 1960s hippiespeak, we were told by a chap called Bill Renfrew who phoned this morning.

"The word Breadhead in this useage probably refers to accountant or money man and is used in a derogatory sense," said Bill. "Then there was an Acidhead, who was someone always high on LSD."

Were we speaking to a hippy who has hung on until the 1990s?

"Er. No," he said. There was a long pause. "Actually, I'm a chartered accountant with American International Group in Hongkong."

A breadhead.

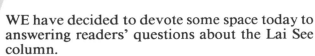

WE have decided to devote some space today to answering readers' questions about the Lai See column.

This is partly to give an insight into the issues of writing this column, but mostly because there was absolutely nothing else to fill this space with today.

Q: Do people really phone you and fax you and write to you all the time with things to put in your column?

A: Well you did, didn't you?

Q: Why is Lai See a "We"? Does he have royal blood?

A: No, we don't have royal blood. So why are we we? The fact is, we feel we would be personalising this column too much if we were an I. It may surprise readers to know there are many difficulties in being a we. For instance, consider references to the spouse. When we first referred to her, we talked about "our wife". "It sounds like I'm being shared. It sounds perverted. What are people going to think?" thundered the lady in question. When we next referred to her, we decided to adhere to grammatical agreements and talked about "our wives". "So who's the other one? It sounds perverted. What are people going to think?" thundered the lady in question. We no longer mention the dear sweet thing.

Saturday 21 APRIL

GOTCHA. We spotted a Hongkong yuppie having an impressively dramatic conversation into his mobile telephone at Joe Bananas in Wan Chai.

"Sell, sell!" he screamed into the telephone.

It was attention-grabbing stuff.

Especially when his telephone started to ring, right in the middle of his "conversation".

Heh heh.

Monday 23 APRIL

THE day passed by uneventfully. At the bar that night, we found Chainsaw looking at a new advertisement for Toyota's new car, the Lexus, which is being imported by Crown Motors, an Inchcape Pacific company.

This car is apparently:

"The most extraordinary car ever built. A car which treats the most advanced automotive technology only as a foundation. Then goes far beyond. Strictly speaking it's probably not even correct to call the Lexus a car anymore. It's gone way past that. It's something else entirely."

The grizzled sub-editor asked: "In that case, surely Lexus is not entitled to the title of Best Car of 1989 given by a magazine, as it claims?"

Tuesday 24 APRIL

NIPPED into Kai Tak Airport to meet someone.
Picked up an airport magazine called *Asia*

Pacific Duty Free.

There we were interested to read that one of the ingredients of that wonderful perfume Hongkong Girl is: "The bouquet of Bohemia, Hongkong's national flower".

Funny. The government has always said Hongkong's national flower was the Bauhinia.

In the encyclopedia it says Bohemia, the name of a region of Czechoslòvakia, gave rise to the word "bohemian" indicating a group of people who are lax about rules and free-thinking.

The perfume people must be right after all. Is it too late to change the flag?

Wednesday 25 APRIL

A HORTICULTURALIST in the territory phoned up to say that Hongkong's "national" flower is actually the Bauhinia Blakeana.

"It is a sterile hybrid," she said.

Coo. Talk about ominous.

Thursday 26 APRIL

YUMMY. This is the menu available today at the Convention Centre in Wan Chai.

Fish
Turkey breast
Pickled kangaroo
Sheep (dry or ready-salted)
Poultry feet
Sheep in brine

However, none of the above is for human consumption. You have to apply it externally to your body.

This is because these are all forms of wearable processed fauna on display at Leather 90, the giant trade fair which started today.

Yes, they'll sell you anything in Hongkong.

NIPPED into the leather fair to check up on sales achieved. Things are not going too well with the Japanese fish leather project, we discovered.

"We're not selling it at the moment," admitted Hiromasa Kikuchi of Yashimoto Hikaku Co of Tokyo.

There have been a few problems. First, the fish skins were not big enough for anything except handbags.

Second, the material was not very strong.

How embarrassing it would be to be stopped on the street and told: "Excuse me, but your personal effects are protruding from that rather fetching garoupa under your arm."

WOKE up bright and early. Well before lunch, in fact.

This was necessary, because we were meeting some of Hongkong's top advertising people for a "Power Lunch" at the Mandarin Grill.

This was a misnomer. So much wine was consumed that participants barely retained enough power to propel themselves towards taxis.

The hot topic was a film called *Crazy People*, in which Dudley Moore plays an advertising man who hits upon the revolutionary idea of telling the truth about his products.

As a result he gets locked up in a mental home.

His slogan for a cigarette company: "Cancer? Perhaps. Flavour? For sure."

Wednesday 2 MAY

CHATTING with Fast Buck in the men's room at the East Point Centre in Causeway Bay, when a classic Hongkong Yuppie arrived in the next stall.

He started dialling his mobile telephone while about to embark upon another quite different activity.

With distinctly unfortunate timing, the person being called responded just when the caller had his hands full with an important matter, so to speak.

The caller had to yell his replies awkwardly into the telephone over the normal sounds of the bathroom.

Not to mention our unsympathetic sniggers over his discomfiture.

Fast Buck, who like us was performing just the one function at a time, said: "No wonder he's worried. He's trying to keep hold of his two most valuable possessions at the same time."

WHEN we got back to the office, had a message to call one of the advertising men we met yesterday.

He said he had always wanted to do "truth-in-advertising." slogans for luxury products, although he knew no-one would ever employ him if he did.

"I have a devastatingly truthful Porsche Design slogan, but don't print my name with it," he said.

The slogan:

"Everyone knows our products are ludicrously overpriced. But admit it, isn't that WHY you buy them?"

"NAAAH. None of that truth-in-advertising stuff could ever happen here in Hongkong. As a matter of fact, we already use more, er, creative licence here than our counterparts in the West anyway," said this morning's caller, another advertising man.

"You mean you tell more lies?" we asked.

"No. Well, not exactly. It's yes and no. Or to put it another way, yes."

Another Hongkong adman, Simon Hayward, creative director of Ball Partnership, called to say (with a touch of wistfulness in his voice): "This truth-in-advertising stuff just goes to show what fun we could have without clients."

Mind you, he wouldn't earn much without clients.

Promising anonymity, we asked several advertisers what slogans they would use for local organisations if they were totally free to speak their minds.

They promised to call back before today's deadline to tell us.

AS six o'clock approached, the phone started to ring. Here are the best three slogans:

Hongkong Urban Taxi Drivers Association: "Most of you cannot afford your own cars. So stop grumbling and pay up."

Svenson Hair Replacement Services:

"Actually, no, we cannot reverse your baldness, but you're so desperate you'll try anything won't you?"

Hongkong Parkview, the apartment complex sitting incongruously in a greenbelt on Hongkong island:

"Everyone's view of a beautiful country park has been spoilt by our luxurious development.

"Except for the lucky people looking out from inside."

Friday 4 MAY

FORMER New China News Agency staffer Tad Stoner told us that when he worked at the Chinese government news agency in Beijing, he and his colleagues used to entertain themselves with a game.

They would make up "truth in advertising" slogans for some of the more prominent mainland companies.

CAAC: "You can't get there from here."

New China News Agency: "That's News To Us."

Tad said: "For the China Travel Service, we had a variation on the government propaganda slogan 'We have friends all over the world'."

This was:

"We have friends all over the world.

"But we don't know how they got there."

Saturday 5 MAY

THE enfante terrible of the advertising scene, Hans Ebert of DDB Needham, came up with three slogans on social and political issues in Hongkong.

For long-suffering Governor Sir David Wilson:

"My hands are tied and my mouth is gagged. So what do you expect me to do or say?"

For Hongkong mobile telephone firms:

"It may be as heavy as a bowling ball, but it is better for posing."

For Hongkong's AIDS awareness campaign: "If you sleep with other people you will get AIDS and die."

"I particularly like that last one," said Hans, a wicked grin lifting his straggly beard. "It's so f***ing blunt."

CHAINSAW Charlie decided to start his work shift with a little witticism of his own.

"Why do they call fast food fast food?" he asked.

Silence.

"Because it is food that makes you wish you were doing a fast. Ha ha ha ha."

Now you see what we have to put up with.

No doubt he had spent hours thinking that one up, as an opener to the "surprising fact" that he was about to unleash upon us: McDonald's is now printing its annual report on old french fries packets and napkins.

Doesn't this make it rather difficult to read?

Not at all, he said. The latest batch of corporate figures have been printed on waste paper recycled from its food outlets.

We called Angela Bassage, who said it was absolutely true. She said she would send us one.

Surely it must smell of old beefburgers?

RECEIVED the McDonald's annual report from Angela Bassage. Took a deep breath.

Yes! It did smell exactly like beefburgers and chips! Was just about to phone Angela and gloat nastily, when we noticed that the business news editor Nick Thompson was messily eating a "double cheeseburger" downwind of our desk.

You cannot get well-bred staff these days.

CHINA business correspondent Geoff Crothall

was just back from the recent Guangzhou Trade Fair. He said he saw a man swimming fully clothed in the unpleasant green waters of Liuhua Park.

Hauled out of the lake by two men in uniforms who demanded to know what he was doing there, he replied: "Washing my clothes."

"He then walked off leaving a trail of green slime behind him," said Geoff.

Clearly, the next five-year modernisation plan had better include coin-operated laundromats in Guangzhou.

Thursday 10 MAY

MS Bassage was on the phone with hot news.

The triumphant team of Chinese, American and Russian climbers that have just conquered Mount Everest are on their way to a reception at the US Consulate in Chengdu in China, she said.

The consul general, Mr Marshall Adair, asked the 51-strong team what they would like to have at the reception.

"Big Macs," they chorused.

"Sure," said Mr Adair.

This proved to be much more problematic than it seemed. You can't just give the recipe to the chef and say: "Rustle up a few of these." And there weren't any McDonald's restaurants in China at the time.

So Mr Adair telephoned McDonald's in Hongkong.

As a result, eight staff and six hundred Big Macs will be winging their way northwards, along with special equipment so they can recreate the, er, dish, in China.

Ms Bassage felt that this was a significant moment in the history of McDonald's conquest of Greater China.

We think the cold air must have gone to everybody's brains.

HAVING lunch with the Fast Buck, we were amazed to hear that Volvo cars, the Swedish firm, is demanding that Hongkong's hostess bar, Club Volvo, gets a new name for itself.

They fear that Hongkong men will confuse the two.

We have always found car salesmen inordinately friendly, but somehow we would never have confused their attentions with those of the young ladies at Club Volvo.

A FINANCIAL gentleman from Wan Chai has sent us a suggestion for a new name for Club Volvo.

He points that that by changing the two vowels in Volvo you can make another word which sounds very similar to the original name, but is a Latinate medical term for a part of the body.

What can he mean?

GOT our latest statement from the Marco Polo Club, for users of Cathay Pacific Airways business class.

We found a little message under the figures.

"Lax service" is the headline, and the note below it talks about the flights between Hongkong and Los Angeles.

We were most impressed by the airline's unusual self-deprecating admission.

Really, we thought the service on trans-Pacific flights has not been all that bad.

HAD a call from someone at Cathay Pacific.

No, the message on our financial statement was not an example of public self-flagellation by Cathay Pacific, she said.

"Lax" is how Los Angeles International Airport likes to describe itself.

In that case, we are most impressed with the humility and honesty shown by the staff at that Californian airport.

NO, no, no, said the next caller. You don't have to think of a new name for Club Volvo at all. The obvious thing to do would be to run the name backwards, and called it Club Ovlov, pronounced Club Of Love.

That's a possibility. Or if they insist on giving it a motoring name, they could call it Club Skoda. The guys there seem to enjoy offbeat publicity.

Monday
14
MAY

IN our pigeon hole this morning there was a letter from a reader about the Trade Department, Spiritual Motherland of the Red Tape Dispenser.

We assumed this would be congratulating them for having given up their bureaucratic rule about combinations of stamps.

But no. It said that thanks to this legendary department, Hongkong is becoming known for making and exporting large numbers of "Mens' Bras".

You might imagine that there were rather wide, flat garments. But the goods are actually rather comely "tank tops" for women.

The skimpy garment, being exported by Hennes and Mauritz, was closer to the classification of "bra" than any other garment on the list, so that's what it had to be called.

But the Trade Department insists on classifying anything that fastens left over right as "men's wear". So they had to be shipped as men's bras.

We are sure the Trade Department means well.

TRIUNE Projects, a firm based in the Sun Hung Kai Centre, Wan Chai, sent us an invitation to visit their stand at the Convention Centre, under the heading: "Verify the best bars in town."

It certainly was the sort of invitation that got our attention. We shall be there to lend our expertise first thing tomorrow.

VISITED the Triune Corp stand at the Convention Centre to "verify the best bars in town".

It was a stall featuring machines that read bar codes.

FAST Buck heard a good joke, inspired by a conversation about investing in art:

Riddle: How many surrealists does it take to screw in a light bulb?

Answer: Eleven. One to wallpaper the giraffe, and ten to fill the bathtub with brightly coloured machine tools.

PLEASED to see that Dr Doom was looking his old bright and cheery self today.

We spotted him across the crowded upper floor at Supatra's restaurant in D'Aguilar Street at lunchtime.

Not only must he be back in business, but he looked so happy that he must have discovered that something really awful must be about to happen to some market or commodity.

A brief conversation after lunch showed that we were right.

"The end has finally come for Hongkong property," he said. "The office market will be the first to be really badly hit, but the disaster will eventually seep into all corners of the property scene in Hongkong."

He said that it was already becoming difficult to fill office blocks with tenants, and the problem would get steadily worse over the next few months.

The good Doctor showed us a complicated report, full of graphs and charts, which made us feel like running to the estate agent to sell office blocks.

And we don't even own one.

WHAT a cheery party we attended at the Bank of China Tower this evening.

It was the official opening bash for the Bank of China's new headquarters, now the tallest building outside North America.

In particularly good spirits were Jeff Finney and his team at the property firm doing the leasing — you know, the one called something like Knight, Kan, Frank, Baillieu, Matthew, Mark, John, Paul and Ringo.

Mr Finney told us he had been fascinated to read the office disaster prediction by Dr Doom in our column yesterday.

He said that he too was willing to stick his neck out — the opposite way. "We predict that property values will go UP by 50 per cent before Christmas," he declared. "What's more, we forecast that the Bank of China Tower will be fully leased by the end of next week."

There was definitely a tone of "Yah-boo-hiss to Dr Doom" in his voice.

Mr Finney is a brave soul. When the bank was being built he would fearlessly stroll around the half-built glass pyramid on top, nonchalantly ignoring the chasm below.

Has he gone out on a limb too far this time?

MR Finney called this morning. "Odd that Dr Doom hasn't replied to my challenge," he said.

A FAX was waiting on our desk when we got back from lunch.

It was a pledge from Dr Doom.

"If, by the end of this week, the Bank of China Tower is fully let as Mr Finney predicts, I shall walk up and down the entire building.

"Moreover, if property values 'go up by 50 per cent before Christmas' as he predicts, I shall WALK UP the entire height of the Bank of China Tower.

"And then I shall JUMP down.

"Best regards, Marc Faber."

We rang Finney's office to tell him the challenge was on, but he was out, no doubt on a selling mission.

He called back an hour later. We read the pledge over the phone to him.

"Oh oh," he said. "I'd better get out there and find some tenants."

He sounded a worried man.

HOW pleasant to start Monday morning with someone else providing the material.

The editor of *Business Traveller* (Asia-Pacific), Mr Vijay Verghese, called to say he got some unusual answers when he asked one of his reporters to check out offbeat gift ideas from Japan. "I'll fax the gift list to you," he said.

Unchi-Kun, the defecating doll (500 yen). You insert a pellet into the, er, "indicated area", light it, and stand back. Hours of fun.

Godzilla toilet paper holder (2,980 yen). Every time you tear off a sheet, it goes "Squawk". The subliminal repercussions defy analysis.

Sushi Clock (8,800 yen). Instead of numbers, there are pieces of wax sushi. It may be 10 past raw tuna (ten past twelve) or sea urchin o'clock (six o'clock).

Marilyn Monroe Bank (3,500 yen) is a doll of the film star straddling a bank. Every time you deposit a coin, a fan blows her dress up. Ideal for bankers.

Tuesday
22
MAY

"DON'T get the idea that it's just the Japanese that are weird," said this morning's first caller.

He was a Hongkong toy industry executive just back from the world toy fair in New York. Most of the world's toys are made by Hongkong companies, in factories just across the border in Guangdong.

One of the biggest attention-grabbers at the show, he said, was a doll called Baby Uh-Oh.

This is the latest incarnation of the "wetsy" doll. This doll, made by Hasbro, automatically stains her nappies in, er, "realistic" shades of yellow and brown. Charming.

She should come with a miniature copy of a certain book by Kathleen Meyer.

Wednesday
23
MAY

AMID all the hustle and bustle at the opening of the international electrical trade show, Elenex

90, today, there was one stand which remained conspicuously untroubled by the presence of visitors, reported Nick Thompson.

The poor representatives from Singapore-based Triad Enterprises, an electronics firm, were at a loss to understand why.

Has nobody had the courage to tell them that "triads" are what Hongkong people call the local mafia?

HAVE been enjoying the Hilton's new worldwide advertising campaign.

This features people in all sorts of exotic locations leaping into taxis and saying "Take me to the Hilton."

Hongkong, unfortunately, must be just too exotic.

At 4 pm we were standing in a taxi queue near Vicwood Plaza in Sheung Wan, when an Australian gentleman reached the front of the queue.

He grandly intoned the actual words of the commercial: "Take me to the Hilton."

The taxi driver who obviously had not been following worldwide developments in advertising, replied:

"No. Too short. Get out of car."

The chap behind him in the queue told him to try getting on a tram.

He probably tried the same line there.

We publicise this purely in support of our truth-in-advertising campaign.

WHO was that tall, pony-tailed figure we spotted lurking around the Bank of China this morning?

Surely it couldn't have been Marc Faber, Dr Doom, checking out how far he has to run up the building, and how far he has to jump down, if he loses his wager?

Or was he satisfying himself that a number of floors of the building were still unoccupied?

Will this same mysterious figure be seen lurking at a parachute or hang-gliding shop later this week?

READING the announcements page to find material for our column, we noted that a limited liability company has applied to have itself registered under the name Hongkong College of Pathologist.

We realise that pathology, the study of disease, is a very specialised subject. But surely there is more than one of you?

IN a sort of "amazing but true" column in the travel section of the *Boston Globe,* we spotted the following: "In Hongkong, goldfish are considered standard office equipment!"

That was it: the complete item.

The headline was possibly misleading: "Sort of Like Paper Clips".

Do the denizens of Boston now believe we use small domestic fish to stick sheets of paper together?

We have never done such a thing, nor heard of anyone else in Hongkong doing so.

TOMORROW we will discover who has won part one of the property wager.

DR Doom has won the first part of his bet. Mr Finney didn't do too badly though.

Two contracts are being discussed on the floors of the Bank of China Tower, but three floors remain empty. He has his fingers crossed over Dr Doom's Christmas Day prediction though.

"Anyone who's prepared to take a running jump off a 70-storey building is definitely taking a short-term view of an approaching market, " he said, referring to the speed at which the pavement would appear to be approaching Dr Faber.

"If he does jump, I'll go up the flagpole and sing *Another One Bites The Dust.*"

It looks as if there could be a lot of interesting activity on the roof of the Bank of China Tower on December 25.

WHAT with all the uncertainty over the Hongkong property market, it seems that there are a lot of salespeople in Hongkong trying to push overseas property.

Some of this is aimed at expats, since they have lots of money, but lack the loyalty factor which would make them buy property here.

Today, we got a missive on this subject from the Hongkong office of Property Search, a Scottish firm run by a Mr Angus Shillingdon.

This talks about overseas property buyers, but describes them in three ways, as "expatriates", "ex-patriots" and "expats".

Deficient spelling? Surely not. How can a company which specialises in expatriate property investment mis-spell the name of their main client base?

Instead, this can only be a subtle classification system which divides their main client base into three groups.

Expatriates — people who work overseas.

Ex-patriots — people who no longer feel nationalistic pride towards their homeland (there's a lot of these in Hongkong).

Ex-Pats — people who were formerly called Pat, but are now called, for example, Melchizadek.

The announcement tells us that the head office is in "Edinburgn."

PEOPLE worried about Hongkong property are not all sending their cash overseas, we learned today from our China correspondent Wang Jinlu.

Much cash, especially from businesses, is expected to find its way up north into the mainland, to a part of Shanghai called Pudong.

This is going to be the "Asian City of the Future" according to the authorities.

Some parts of China are really coming along rather well.

Mentioned the Pudong area in the bar that night, only to find it raised inexplicable sniggers from the Americans in attendance.

Saturday 2 JUNE

BUMPED into Don Cohn, an American writer-translator working in Hongkong.

He said the Chinese authorities would get a strange response if they tried marketing this "city of the future" with that name overseas.

The pronunciation of Pudong (*pu dong* means River East in Mandarin) is very similar to Podunk, a most uncomplimentary slang term in America.

He said: "The reaction would be: 'Look, honey, they's got a podunk in China now, and they want us to invest in it. Ha ha ha ha ha."

We looked it up on Webster's, and found that it meant: "A small town or village considered as backward, dull and insignificant."

THAT night at JJ's we mentioned the Pudong/Podunk problem to Chainsaw.

He said he already knew about it, having many relatives in the US.

"There are actually two real-life Podunks in America, one in Massachusetts and one in Connecticut," he said. "You don't hear much about them because nobody admits they live there."

Monday 4 JUNE

THIS is it. It's arrived. This is the first anniversary of That Day. The Day Hongkong Got the Willies.

Got to the office early, listened to the radio and peered out of the window. But there didn't seem to be anything going on.

This is the day that has been described by our cousins over the fence as the June 4 "incident", "event", "occurrence", "happening", and even "accident". ("Whoops! Sent in the tanks. Silly us." Sound of slapped forehead.)

Oddly enough, looking back from this perspective, it is surprising how little major financial damage it did to Hongkong.

It would be really interesting to know what the Hongkong business community's real attitude to all this is now, one year on.

LATER in the day, decided to call Wang Jinlu in Beijing to find out if anything had happened in Tiananmen Square.

"The only thing that reporters could get access to was the Mao-soleum, so I went in there," he said.

He passed through the halls and shuffled passed the mortal remains of Chairman Mao Zedong (which now have a greenish tinge), before entering the gift shop at the back.

"Lo and behold, the shop was featuring toy tanks, complete with Chinese military insignia and flashing lights in the gun barrels. I asked if they had any toy students to go with the toy tanks. They didn't."

He paused. "Then I decided to turn the tank over. Guess what it said on the back? 'Made in Hongkong'."

Well, that seems to answer this morning's question.

Tuesday
5
JUNE

CALLED a few other friends in the mainland (being careful to avoid the now unphoneable Shanghai) to see if anything was going on elsewhere in China.

The Shandong correspondent was the only one having a bit of excitement. But it was nothing to do with the democracy movement.

"You really should pop into the coastal city of Weihai and go around sniffing a few of the inhabitants," he said. "The city is holding a "pretty city" tourism promotion featuring clean citizens." Officials have undertaken to teach "every resident a strong sense of hygiene and public health".

It sounded wonderful. The scrubbed and fresh-smelling citizenry are the high point of a campaign that includes more predictable steps, such as distributing 100,000 potted plants around the streets.

He had heard that Mr Chen Minzhang, Minister of Public Health, is so impressed that he hopes to launch a China-wide campaign for clean cities filled with clean people.

Chainsaw commented that there was "a touch of the Lady Macbeth about all this".

Wednesday
6
JUNE

HAD a mournful lunch with the boss of a construction firm.

He was saying it was terrible the number of engineers Hongkong was losing through the brain drain.

Especially since we will need more than ever before to build the new airport and docks.

Back in the office, we told Chainsaw Charlie we planned to write an article about low morale among engineers.

"Utter rubbish," he said. "They LOVE the brain drain. It's pushing up all their wages."

His cynicism is sometimes rather tiresome.

We know several engineers, and we are convinced the members of this noble profession are solely concerned about the negative effects of the brain drain on our beloved homeland.

Thursday
7
JUNE

WHY has someone at the Hongkong Institute of

Engineers provided the publishers of *The Emigrant* magazine with their mailing list?

The magazine is using this list to send out mail order passport information, we discovered this morning when someone sent us some computer-labelled envelopes as evidence.

The publishers have not even bothered to eliminate the engineers' membership numbers from the institute's labels on the letters.

Sometimes we get the feeling we are not all pulling together against the brain drain problem.

HAD a call from Wang Jinlu that evening. What he told us made us think that perhaps China is not, after all, on the brink of becoming a modern industrial country with a city of the future on its shoulder.

Organisers of the Asian Games in Beijing sent out thousands of homing pigeons to train them.

Hardly any arrived.

Investigators found more than 100 people standing in fields with rifles waiting for their lunch to fly over.

"It beats queuing outside the butcher's," said Wang.

Anyway, it shows the existence of a healthy entrepreneurial spirit. There is still hope.

Friday 8 JUNE

POPPED in to see Hongkong human resources specialist Mike Minty to get some feedback on the staff shortage situation around town.

We found him having an attack of anti-yuppyism.

"The blasted things are everywhere. You cannot escape them. Mobile phones," he explained.

Mr Minty told us he had just been strolling down a side-street in Western District, when he came across a shop making imitation mobile telephones for the spirit world, for sale at HK$30 each.

"When someone dies, you buy one and burn it, and a corresponding real one will appear in heaven or wherever the deceased ends up," he said.

IN a state of deepening gloom, we went to a seminar on Hongkong's Financial Future.

But it was not the sort of depressing thing one might expect what with 1997 in the offing — not at all. Several speakers were most bullish, including David Li, boss of the Bank of East Asia.

Mind you, we felt sorry for Patrick Thomas, the capital markets specialist, who was looking a bit uncomfortable when he got up to make his contribution.

"I would like to thank David Li for getting me out of bed early on a Saturday morning, and making me make a presentation immediately after a real live professor and two other distinguished speakers, who have effectively blown my prepared text to smithereens," he said. "I hope you were all enjoying your coffee while I rewrote my speech."

What a way to start the weekend.

GOT up early to do some gift shopping before work. Father's Day next weekend.

In Mannings in Exchange Square we found a special offer in the male cosmetics section. On the Brut counter, there was a "Triad Gift Set" at HK$157.

This includes a bottle of eau de cologne,

aftershave creme lotion and deodorant stick.

Clearly it is a selection of shaving accessories for people who have their own sharp instruments.

WHEN we got to our offices in Quarry Bay, we mentioned to our sub-editor that we thought it a bit naughty for a drugstore to honour the secretive Chinese mafia in this way. Their existence was supposed to be illegal, after all.

"Nonsense," he said. "Why should they be left out of the festivities? Many triads are family men. Besides, wouldn't you rather have nice-smelling triads around then sweaty ones?"

We suppose there is a sort of logic to that.

Chainsaw added: "I think you should phone Mannings and advise them to do it properly: stock up on manicure sets for shaping fingernails, right-hand white gloves, symbolic red poles, drinking straws and kitchen knives. A festive meat cleaver would go down well."

Tuesday 12 JUNE

WANG Jinlu rang to tell us that the New China News Agency was running a terribly interesting piece about the mass production of dogs in Kunming.

Breeders have turned out 12,105 in the past 30 years, mainly for crook-catching, he said.

One dog caught an armed burglar after racing down four roads and leaping two walls. It was awarded a Third Class Citation of Merit.

The dog was called Black Wind, although the report didn't say why.

Wednesday 13 JUNE

CHINA business writer Geoff Crothall strolled

into the office and threw his fedora onto the computer.

"Wang forgot to mention something," he said. "Kunming city, capital of Yunnan province, south west China, is famed for something else involving dogs. Kunming is the centre of China's dog stew industry."

He told us that roasted or broiled Kunming dogs produce dark meat with a rich flavour, usually spiced with chillis and eaten with rice. It was an interesting culinary experience, he said.

He didn't say anything about "black wind" either.

Thursday
14
JUNE

HAD to call Fast Buck when we saw the report on the wires this morning.

If he thinks Hongkong people and the Taiwanese are commercially a bit "sharp", he should check out the people of the Philippines.

Somebody has been selling off chunks of Manila Airport.

This is rather embarrassing because the airport is owned by the government.

Airport management had to take out newspaper advertisements to tell people who had paid for deeds to the airport that they were counterfeit.

The American corporate financier was suitably impressed.

"Now that the idea has been circulated, better keep a close eye on Kai Tak Airport," he said.

Friday
15
JUNE

LUNCH today was the high point of the week. We had salmon steak in champagne sauce at the Excelsior Grill Room with a rather attractive lady executive friend called Ms Chiu.

She told us that after lunch she was heading out to buy a fur coat. Apparently they are cheaper in summer.

"Aren't you worried about animal rights activists?" we asked.

"No," she said. She had heard of a new type of "safe" fur coat.

"They are now making reversible fur coats, which look like normal cloth coats on one side. But when you arrive at your destination, you turn them inside out to reveal them to be mink or sable coats."

MS Chiu called in the morning to say that she had had problems choosing her coat. "I wanted them all," she said.

The fur makers were even more devious than she expected.

"They are now making furs which look like fakes — except for the price tags," she enthused.

One Hongkong furrier had told her about a US designer who had just launched a collection he called "real fake fur".

These coats — which cost up to US$10,000 — look like fakes, so a wearer can promenade down the street without worrying about being spat on or being splashed with red paint. Some of the coats even look like real plastic.

We were most impressed by this concept, and immediately started writing an article about it for our column on Monday.

JUST as we were sneaking out of the office, our eagle-eyed sub-editor called us back. He had spotted a flaw in the argument in our fur exclusive.

"Why would anyone spend US$10,000 for a mink coat in order for it to look like a fake? All you'd have to do is buy a REAL fake one that looks even MORE like a fake for HK$300," said Chainsaw.

He had a good point there. We wonder if the fur industry has really thought this one through.

STARTED the week by nipping into a new fashion shop called Liaison on Wyndham Street.

One of the marketing lines for its main product range, Moonline Bags, is: "Buy it and look smarter than you really are."

This is the first time we have seen marketing specialists deliberately targeting that large but hitherto ignored market segment, Incredibly Stupid Consumers.

Clearly an innovative step that will surely increase turnover.

THE Stock Market of Hongkong called to say that the results of a survey of the investment scene were to be announced tomorrow.

The only finding the caller would leak was that the typical Hongkong investor is a thirty-something man who wears a white collar.

This is not terribly surprising. A Moonline Bags customer could have worked that one out.

But it is a jolly good thing the stock exchange researchers did not do the survey in May and June last year, when the market crashed because of student demonstrations in China.

The conversation would have gone like this:

Market researcher: Are you blue-collar or white-collar?

Investor: I've lost my shirt. We've all lost our shirts.

GOT to the stock market early and sat for a moment by the fountains outside, watching the Star Ferry ply from side to side of the harbour.

What a fine complex Exchange Square is.

A pity everything in it is designed in circles. Clearly some mis-translation in the original plans.

Entering the conference room, we were handed a copy of the survey by debonair if skinny stock exchange chief Francis Yuen himself.

He revealed that the fastest-growing portion of new entrants to the world of making share money grow (well, okay, change size) are women. New investors are younger than past ones and are starting from a low personal income bracket.

So who are the members of this new generation − of young, lower-income females? Where are they hiding out?

GOT back to the South China Morning Post Building to find our secretary reading the *Financial Times.*

You don't think . . . ?

Surely not.

THE gloomy atmosphere at the FCC at lunch could only mean one thing: a journal had gone bust.

"The business magazine *Billion* has folded," said our neighbour at the bar. ("Folded" is journalists' jargon for "finished for good" as in "I folded a bottle of scotch last night.")

"Mind you," he added, "there's a rumour that the publisher may put out a slimmed down version."

"Good idea. You could call it *Million* or *Quite a Lot, Really,*" we suggested. They didn't seem to appreciate the idea.

BUMPED into advertising man Hans Ebert in JJ's in the evening.

Boy, was he angry. The hirsuite ad-man's television commercial for the "Right of Abode" cause was tipped to be a big winner at the 4As this year — the Annual Advertising Academy Awards.

But the judges disqualified it since it was not shown as a paid advertisement. The television stations thought it too political and only transmitted it as a news item.

Hans, a man of passion, was positively seething.

Saturday
23
JUNE

CRAWLED out of bed reluctantly to attend a press conference by the world's largest energy company.

At least it was at the Mandarin Oriental hotel, so the coffee was good.

Unfortunately Electricite de France chairman Pierre Delaporte was a French speaker who does not speak English.

The audience were Cantonese speakers who did not speak French.

At first, they tried to make a go of it by using an interpreter who spoke French and English — but she did not understand technical terms, so the conference descended into embarrassed muttering.

Then the firm's Far East director Vincent de Rivaz stepped into the breach.

He was a French speaker who could manage English only avec un top 'eavy Frensshh accente, si vous knows what nous means.

So it ended up with a French speaker trying to communicate Mandarin names such as Xiamen in broken Franglais-style English to Cantonese listeners.

By this stage, everyone was so confused that nobody had the slightest idea what language they were listening to, or indeed, what their own names were.

Bon chance avec le power station, monsieurs.

That was an even worse way to start a weekend.

FAST Buck told us over dinner at the Eagle's Nest that many foreign investors were still unwilling to put their cash into Hongkong firms.

"Local secretaries and taxi-drivers may be buying shares, but foreigners feel that Hongkong public companies are not run in an open and straightforward way, in the way implied by the word 'public'," he said.

A company director dining with us replied: "Nonsense. They are as accessible as public firms anywhere."

"They why do so many of them have ex-directory phone numbers?" asked Fast Buck. It's true, you know.

Monday 25 JUNE

NOT a lot of news about today. Only interesting thing was a report from the consumer electronics show in Chicago. For people who throw scrunched up balls of paper into wastepaper bins, there is a basketball-type hoop to stick on your bin. It cheers when you score.

Talking Tissue is an electronic toilet tissue roller. Every time you use it, it makes a comment, such as: "Nice one." (A good one for our Japanese friends).

The new Polite Telephones will not go drrrrng drrrrrng or blleeeet blleeeeet. When someone calls, the telephone will speak to you. It will slinkily purr: "Darling, pick up the phone."

Of course, we could always train the Business Post secretary to do the same.

POPPED out to visit some contacts. In his little office in Yee Wo Street, Causeway bay, Five-Finger Wu had come up with his greatest discovery yet: nuclear fission in a suppository.

The Atomic Enema is now appearing on shelves throughout the territory, courtesy of Benzene Chem and Pharm Ltd.

US scientists may claim to have done it in a jam jar, but our boys have done it in a tiny plastic container inserted in a very small space indeed.

The box was illustrated with all sorts of molecule-like diagrams, but Wu was disappointed to find that there was no explanation about how the nuclear reaction in the enema actually functions.

We don't know how it works, but we DEFINITELY wouldn't want to be standing near to anyone using one.

Tuesday 26 JUNE

WE trekked to the lower reaches of darkest Yau Ma Tei today, in search of the Hotel Fortuna, where Wing On Holdings was having a shareholders' meeting.

But alas, there was no room at the inn for the press. We were all made to sit in a separate room away from the fun.

The firm's public relations staff handed out

typed sheets to read, and distributed custard tarts for mollification purposes.

We almost dropped ours on our Gieves and Hawkes trousers when we realised that this amazing document was a record of all the decisions taken at the meetings — which was only then about to begin.

It was clearly a remarkable work of forecasting which should rank with the prophecies of Nostradamus.

The document revealed that a quorum would turn up, all resolutions would be passed, and a general mandate would be given to the directors to issue and sell extra shares.

AND this, dear reader, is exactly what happened.

At least, we think it is. After a long wait, we were ushered into a different room on the other side of the building and told to wait.

Fifteen minutes later, the public relations girl announced that all the directors had left the building so we might as well go home.

We could only deduce that staff had accidentally put us in the wrong room and the directors had accidentally made a speedy exit, thus accidentally depriving reporters of a chance of speaking to them.

A CALLER from Europe said he had had a letter from a Hongkong company asking him to send diseased pieces of cow to the Far East in exchange for cash.

Could this be legitimate?

Yes, we said.

Clearly the gallstone kings of Kowloon are stepping up their business. The family of Mr Poon King-kee have long been spreading the word that rural people around the world can get rich quick by cutting up any dead cows that they may have lying around. Any gallstones found should be sent to the Poons' company, Alice Import-Export of Kimberly Road, Kowloon. These are used for aphrodisiac purposes.

(It is a bit of a messy job since only one in a hundred cows has them.)

The marketing letter, going out to newspapers all over the world, is signed by Ms Josephine Poon, daughter of the boss.

"There is an exciting news release for your esteemed paper which will make your readers jump for joy," it says.

"Make money from product which normally people throw away. Get rich is always news, great news!"

Hmmm. We are not sure that this presents the most positive image of Hongkong people as sensitive individuals with poetic souls, but never mind.

DID any readers do some home surgery on domestic animals after reading yesterday's column?

Reader Robert Jones, who knows about these things, sent some pointers.

Don't go expecting gallstones attached to the main bladder, which is a urinary bladder. You will end up no richer, and probably smell pretty awful. Check out a smaller bladder nearby. If your domestic pet is a rat, don't bother, he writes. Rats have no gall bladders. Happy slashing.

BOY were those minority shareholders steaming

today at the end of the meetings of the Lau brothers firms. You could almost smell the smoke wafting from their ears as they stomped out of the get-togethers at the Mandarin Oriental hotel.

One shareholder asked whether the brothers were entitled to a listing in the Guinness Book of Records for overpaying themselves.

Others cooked up a scheme to influence the activities of Joseph and Thomas Lau, the mega-rich brothers who run the Evergo group.

The minority shareholders plan to conjure up the forces of ancient Chinese magic — a curse called Da Siu Yahn.

ON the way back, nipped in to see Five-Finger Wu in Causeway Bay, who was very familiar with Da Sui Yahn.

This is how you do it.

You inscribe the name and date of birth (according to the traditional Chinese calendar) of a person on a piece of paper cut into the shape of a doll.

The doll is then taken to a group of practitioners of the mystic arts.

"Some of these rather sweet little old ladies can be found under the flyover by Canal Road East in Wan Chai," he said.

The ladies beat the paper dolls violently with their slippers. As a result, ancient magic affects the people represented by the dolls.

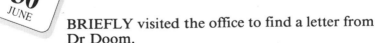

BRIEFLY visited the office to find a letter from Dr Doom.

"The claim of an employee of the real estate broker Knight Kan Frank Baillieu four weeks ago to lease out all the vacant space in the Bank of China Tower in one week was obviously hot air and had no substance," it said.

"Several entire floors are still empty. Maybe the Ladies Recreation Club could take up several floors for indoor tennis courts?"

AT lunch, one stockbroker at Brown's today told us that he considered the Da Siu Yahn rather far-fetched.

We icily pointed out that this was rather rich coming from a man who trusts his fortune to technical analysis. That shut him up.

CALLED the office from the bedside to see if anything was happening.

There was a letter from Hongkong's literary agents, Chris and Stephanie Holmes of Imprimatur, we were informed by the Business Post secretary.

Hoped it was a promise to publish our novel, if and when we ever write one. Decided to go into the office to check.

IN fact, it turned out to be a bit of news about a new book: *Chung Kuo* by David Wingrove, a novel about China in the future, published by New English Library.

"But who should we find featured in this dramatic page-turner?" asked Chris, who is heavily into rhetorical questions.

"A Far Eastern businessman called . . . Hans Ebert," he answered himself. "The odd thing is the personality attributed to this man with the unusual name: he is brash, hot-headed, fiery and so on."

Most curious. This can only be a reference to Hongkong's own Hans Ebert, highly flammable creative boss of advertising agency DDB Needham.

We called Ebert's office and his home for a comment, but he was nowhere to be found.

Tuesday 3 JULY

MANAGED to track down Hans Ebert, who was in his recording studio, no doubt laying some advertising jingle we will all be humming soon.

We showed him passages from the book.

Page 116 went on at length about Hans Ebert's rudeness and his arrogant assumption that he could have anything he wanted, by simply buying it.

Page 128 said: "Ebert had a reputation for being headstrong. For doing what others would never dare to do. But it was understandable. He had been born to rule."

There were many others in the same vein.

Hans was almost speechless (yes, yes, we know that's hard to believe).

"It's amazing. It's so . . . TRUE," he gasped. Coincidence? No way.

"It is obvious that this man has been reading about my fight to get my Right of Abode ad back on TV, and he has probably been talking to my clients."

He took another look at the harsh picture painted in the references. "Or perhaps my ex-clients."

Wednesday 4 JULY

STAYED up late last night reading *Chung Kuo.*
They are now cloning Hans Eberts.

But the real one (in the book, that is) has discovered a difference between himself and the replicas. They have a black lacquered hip-flask where his liver should be.

This morning, we told the real one about this, and he said he liked the idea. "Excellently conceived optional extra," he said. "Does it say how to spot a real Hans Ebert from a fake?"

We flicked through the pages.

"Yes," we replied. There is something "too animated" about the speech and gestures of the cloned robots. And it has strangely burning eyes.

We didn't tell him, but the Hongkong one sounds extraordinarily like a clone.

Thursday 5 JULY

FINALLY got to the end of the book in the early hours of this morning. Quite a good read.

It is possible that the bosses of the real Hans at DDB Needham may be given an idea by this.

The clones cost one million yuan to make. An absolute bargain, what with executive salaries these days.

They could order a half dozen and then Ball Partnership, Leo Burnett, Ogilvy and Mather and the others had better watch out.

Boy, we would HATE to be among the judges at the 4As, when half a dozen Eberts are out baying for revenge.

Friday 6 JULY

FAST Buck was on the phone. He had just come

back from a business trip to Taipei.

"Asia is slowly but surely getting a social conscience," he said. The Government of Taiwan had just ordered the makers of the country's most popular cigarette to change the brand name.

"They are called 'Long Life'," said Buck. "The Government reckons that's a misleading name for a cigarette."

AT 4.10 pm, Chainsaw Charlie came hiccupping back from a long and merry lunch. We mentioned this to him, since he is good at snappy titles.

"Hmm," he said. "Long Life, huh? Easy. How about Lung Lifeless?"

Monday 9 JULY

ONE of the wonderful things about Hongkong is that it is a meeting place for so many contrasting influences. It is more than just East meets West. Old traditional Chinese wisdom is meeting Hongkong's own up-and-coming yuppie Asian trends.

We were reminded of this when we received our copy of Albert Cheng's monthly magazine, *Hongkong,inc.*

Although this is a serious business journal, as one might find anywhere, it also features an updated version of a traditional Chinese Tung Sing almanac in each issue.

This is labelled:

"The Wonderful Glorious Calendar as used by businessmen from Li Ka-shing to a street hawker. Now you know what your competitor is up to."

Pretty impressive stuff.

Since Mr Li, supposedly the richest man in Hongkong, allegedly uses it, we have determined to give it a go ourselves.

CONSULTED the businessman's almanac as soon as we got into the office.

Today one should demolish one's dwelling, it said.

Hmm. Swire Properties would surely have something to say if we knocked down our building in Causeway Bay.

Of course it's easy for someone like Li Ka-shing to have skyscrapers knocked down on a whim, but it's a damn sight more difficult for the rest of us.

NOTHING in the almanac for today. Our failure to demolish our building had no ill effects that we can see.

DISCOVERED at the bar that the latest trendy cocktail is called the Exxon Valdez.

It's a glass of blue curacao with a splash of black rum. The rum floats on top and looks like an oil slick.

How do you drink it? On the rocks of course.

ROUND the back of the FCC bar, we bumped into Hongkong film man Russell Cawthorne.

He was bursting with excitement about Golden Harvest's successful Teenage Mutant Ninja Turtles film.

"Don't get your nunchakas in a knot, but I can tell you a secret. At the great personal risk of being shredded in a shower of shirikins, I can now tell you that Golden Harvest is preparing to film a sequel. It doesn't have a title yet, but I am putting in a strong recommendation for Turtle Recall."

But what are nunchakas and shirikins?

"They are ninja weapons. Do you mean to say that you don't have any in your office? I have several in mine."

So that's why minions at Golden Harvest work so hard.

STARTED the day with the businessman's almanac.

Today we should ideally be occupied with erecting a pillar.

But we should be careful not to buy a field, it said.

Couldn't quite see how to manage the first instruction, but were proud to say we followed the second to the letter.

FELT like a holiday, so we called our travel agents, Love and White of Des Voeux Road, to see what they could offer.

They put us on hold and played a tune to us. It was: *There's No Place Like Home.*

Later, we called the Hongkong Tourist Association to get some ideas from them. They also put us on hold. They played: *Home, Home On The Range.*

Clearly, there are some higher forces in operation here, persuading us to stay where we are.

HAD a quick glance at the almanac as soon as we got into Quarry Bay, since Friday the 13th is supposedly an unlucky day.

It said we must resist the temptation to dig a well or build a pond, however hard that may be.

Not exactly a much of a challenge, is it?

OKAY, so who is the joker who chose the telephone tune to entertain callers to the Border Division Headquarters of the Royal Hongkong Police?

These are the over-worked gentlemen who spend much of their time dealing with the forced repatriation of illegal immigrants.

The chosen song is *Greensleeves,* which goes: "Alas, my love, you do me wrong, to cast me off discourteously."

AT the bar at Soho discotheque that night, we got talking to Chainsaw Charlie about this almanac. The reason it wasn't working, he said, was that we were taking it at face value.

"You have to interpret the instructions yourself to make them relevant to the modern day," he said.

We pulled it out of our briefcase and had a look at the recommendations for the rest of the week. Sunday looked odd.

"It is a bad day for fixing sauces and travelling to distant lands." What can that mean?

"It's easy," said Chainsaw. "You shouldn't eat any airline food tomorrow, because it will be a rotten day for airline caterers."

Thursday next week, July 19 (the only day this month designated as a good day for taking a bath), the serious adherent will be rearing cattle.

Tuesday, July 31, (the only day this month designated as a good day for eating vegetarian food), he will be busy building himself a Taoist altar.

Even our esteemed headline-writer was nonplussed at all this.

He summarily inhaled a triple scotch and said: "Well obviously the image of Hongkong yuppies living gentrified lives in tower blocks does not apply to everyone."

Monday 16 JULY

THE Spanish Environmental and Pollution Control Trade Mission will be in Hongkong today, says the news diary.

We hope they did not fly in yesterday and eat airline food on the way.

The advance publicity is intriguing.

One firm represented deals in "activated sludge for food industries". We can only assume this is something to do with fast food.

Another makes "fabrics, sacks and bags for vet filtration". How one filters veterinarians or why they need to be filtered, we have no idea.

The most intriguing is a firm which handles "hospitable waste".

We can only assume that this is a reference to something like Smoky Mountain, the garbage hill on which people live in Manila.

Tuesday 17 JULY

THIS anti-pollution bandwagon is getting an increasing number of jumpers-on.

In the mail today was a product announcement from the British Trade Commission in Hongkong about a device to reduce noise pollution from guns. It has the delightfully gentle name of "the Hushpower".

"Hushpower silencers can be supplied ready fitted to a single barrel gun or added as a conversion to any suitable semi-automatic or pump-action shotgun," it says.

We cannot see why the British Trade Commission, which is going to be expanded into a full British Consulate in 1997, is trying to sell gun silencers.

Is this normal for consulates?

THERE was a classified advertisement in the *South China Morning Post* today for an "Artificial Flower Merchandiser" required by a Japanese firm in Central.

The applicant must have at least two years of experience in artificial flower fields, it says.

That's silly. Everyone knows they make them in factories.

THE Lamma Looker called in the early evening to say he was much intrigued by the cargo he saw on the Yung Shue Wan ferry at 4.30 pm from Central.

It was a consignment of cardboard food boxes labelled "Professional Chicken".

"Was this special fodder for the increasing number of yuppies on Lamma Island?" he asked. "Or is it a type of chicken that takes the whole business of being a chicken very seriously?"

HORRIFIED to hear that Hongkong has been declared a no-go area for the re-issue of credit cards by the UK-based Co-op Bank, who broke the bad news in a letter to local lecturer Veronica Pearson.

Has the territory's reputation overseas deteriorated that much?

A HOLDER of an Access card from the UK told us that he had been told his card would not be renewed — and he was a man who used to accidentally over-pay his credit card bills. Something odd going on with British banks.

MET Sheung Wan writer Neal McGrath in the FCC that night.

He also wanted to have a go at foreign banks.

"Have you seen the great new security product now available from the Citibank Card Products centre in Hongkong?" he asked.

He showed us the brochure. The "Untouchable Safe" is a safe in which you can put all your "dearest valuables". But it looks exactly like a hi-fi stereo amplifier.

Neal said: "The unsuspecting criminal may think he's only stealing a measly little stereo amplifier, but what he doesn't know — hah! — is that you've cleverly hidden your valuables inside."

They could follow it up with a safe disguised as a video player, or a jewellery box, or even a gold ingot, he enthused.

We definitely detected a note of sarcasm in his voice.

We wonder if the Citibank products centre has really thought this one through.

Monday 23 JULY

OH dear. Got into the office this morning to find the news that yet another Hongkong customer of a British bank has had a letter informing him that his credit card cannot be reissued to this financially dangerous territory.

Only this gentleman's name just happens to be Mr A.W. Nicolle.

That's right, Tony Nicolle, Hongkong's Commissioner of Banking, the top banking official in the territory, has been told he cannot have a bank credit card. Now is that a gross international *faux pas* or what?

MR Nicolle has not taken this insult lying down. He told us he had taken up the matter with authorities at his bank in the UK.

The bemused banking chief explained who he was, and what the situation really was in Hongkong.

"Dodgy? Hongkong? No way!" was the gist of his argument, although he delivered it in rather more elegant language.

Mr Nicolle's UK bank manager replied: "I would concede that we have been arguably over-cautious as far as Hongkong is concerned." He agreed to send the banking commissioner a new card.

"One has to stand up and be counted," Mr Nicolle told us.

International perception of Hongkong is clearly suffering.

MEANWHILE, the rehabilitation of China in the world community continues apace, reported a reader on a crackly phone line from Guangzhou.

"The authorities are taking an odd sort of marketing angle, though," he said. "It is on the lines of: 'Come to sunny China. Ride a tank. Fire real weapons. Use the People's Liberation Army firing range.'"

The tourist department in Qingyuan town is offering a military sightseeing tour.

This includes a visit to Huangpu Military Academy, where you can ride tanks and use weapons, he said.

We would have thought it would be better to try to dissociate China and tanks in the minds of tourists, but then, they are the experts.

Thursday 26 JULY

HAD a call from Wang Jinlu in Beijing. He agreed that the 'ride a tank' idea wasn't such a great marketing angle.

"But officials here are hoping the Asian Games should get a lot of positive attention, overseas and locally," he said.

Millions of Beijing citizens are going to take part in a quiz on the Asian Games called "Asian Games On My Mind".

Wang said: "The questions are all on, er, interesting topics connected with the games, such as 'The Standard of Behaviour Required by Local Residents During the Event'."

"Come off it. If you have to work six days a week to make a few renminbi, why would anyone waste their time answering questions like that?"

"Members of the Beijing Municipal Trade Union will for a start. It has ordered them to do so," he said.

Friday 27 JULY

THE brain drain is speeding up. Word was out at the Hongkong Press Club today about an increasingly fashionable way of leaving your job.

They call it the Kai Tak Farewell.

It almost always happens on the last day of the month. The employee collects his salary cheque as early as possible in the day, cashes it, and then phones in from Kai Tak Airport to tell the boss he has resigned.

"Some do it to avoid any possible hassles with broken contracts. Others just don't want to pay their tax bills," said a source at a Kowloon Bay company which has suffered several Kai Tak Farewells recently.

The following conversation occurred between

his boss and an employee resigning on the telephone from the airport.

Boss: Is it the money? If it is just the money, I am sure we can come to some arrangement.

Ex-employee: It's too late for that now.

Boss: It's not too late. I can arrange that right away.

Ex-employee: It is too late. I've already gone through immigration.

AUGUST in Hongkong. The humidity is at 99 per cent. The walls drip like scenery from the film Alien. The electricity shorts itself out with an angry buzz every other day.

Everything leather in the flat and the office grows a layer of furry orange mould.

With the notable and highly suspicious exception of that "guaranteed real leather" sofa we bought cut-price in Taikoo Shing in spring.

An eerie silence descends on Hongkong. This is all relative, of course.

What we mean is that there are only five jackhammers going in our corner of Causeway Bay, rather than the normal nine.

Not much news about at the moment, since all the newsmakers, criminals, business people, etc, seem to have gone off on their hols. Unfortunately, this means we all have to work extremely hard to fill the newspaper.

"Filling the newspaper every day during the silly season is one of the true challenge of daily journalism," said Chainsaw. "It separates genuine reporters from idle hacks who can only re-hash press releases."

We have decided to apply for a vacation.

Friday 3 AUGUST

THE first caller today was an emigration consultant from Silvercord House, Tsim Sha Tsui.

"I don't know whether to laugh or cry," he said. He had been busy negotiating with the Immigration Department on his client's pending departure from Hongkong.

Then he received a letter from a different officer. So he rang the department and said: "What's this all about? The other chap said it was all sorted out. Can you check?"

"There are no notes left on file about the case."

"Can't you just walk over and ask him?"

"No, I can't."

"Why not?"

Ominous silence.

"Er. He's emigrated to Canada."

It's really rather frightening.

Sunday 5 AUGUST

ON the way to the brunch buffet at the FCC, we noticed a large crowd outside the Hongkong bank headquarters.

Crowds stopped to watch as some sort of dance show was filmed by TV crews around the back of the bank.

This consisted of large numbers of young Hongkong gentlemen leaping around energetically in black suits and white gloves.

A pair of British touroids stopped near us to ogle at the spectacle.

"What's going on, dear?" asked the wife.

"It's the triads — the Chinese mafia," explained the husband knowingly.

Now we are fully aware that Hongkong's underworld triad scene is distressingly close to the surface at times.

But formation dancing in the streets? We haven't QUITE reached that stage, thank you very much.

One would think that Hongkong society is totally disintegrating in the face of 1997, the way some people go on.

Tuesday 7 AUGUST

UNDERWORLD elements in Kowloon have embarked upon one of the strangest money-making rackets yet.

They are selling flowers in a threatening manner.

Yes, we know it sounds unlikely, but we heard this today from an educated Chinese business-woman who was accosted by a flower-wielding gang in Hunghom.

She parked her car near a funeral parlour in the area, and was approached by flower-sellers who demanded that she buy their goods. She replied that she had already bought flowers for the funeral she was attending.

Then they became abusive and menacing. "They were clearly an organised business," she said. About 45 minutes later, she left the funeral and a rock was thrown at her car. "The whole thing was a nightmare," she said.

This place is falling to bits.

What next? Extortion by charity collectors?

"EXCUSE me, sir," said a policeman-like voice on the telephone. "You know you said in your column yesterday that one day there might be extortion by charity workers in Hongkong? Well, we've already got that," said the owner of the voice, who happened to be a policeman.

Police are now in the middle of an investigation of "flag-selling with menaces" in a Sha Tin district housing estate, he explained.

The flags were made for a normal flag day. But the following Saturday, someone turned up with a large number of unsold flags.

Strongarm tactics were used by burly "charity" collectors to unload the collection on residents. Remarkably high prices were achieved.

How shocking. What next? Sampan women holding tourists to ransom?

"EXCUSE me," said the woman on the phone. "But I've been held to ransom by sampan skippers."

Several callers said the same. A party heading out from the Sea Ranch settlement to Cheung Chau island at the weekend got into a dispute over fees. The boat came to a halt.

Only when a satisfactory amount of cash had been raised did the boat travel on to Cheung Chau.

What next? Priests using handguns to increase the takings on their collection plates?

Friday 10 AUGUST

NO parishioners called about their priests today, thank God.

Saturday 11 AUGUST

HAD lunch at the Grand Hyatt with an advertising executive called Chris, nicknamed Bowtie.

He said we should use our column to warn businesses in Hongkong about the escalation in junk mail operations.

"There are some rather dodgy ones going around. All they care about is getting business, and there are certain shortcomings in their methods," he said. "I took out a subscription to a Hongkong business magazine, and then another one as a gift for a girlfriend."

The young lady shortly started receiving the magazine with a label saying: "This comes to you from Chris Bowtie."

Mr Bowtie's expression hardened. "But then, a few weeks later, she started to get junk mail — tons of it.

"And every single piece of junk mail had a label saying: 'This comes to you from Chris Bowtie.' I contacted the magazine company, but to no avail."

His eyes misted over: "As you can imagine, this was the cause of several arguments between myself and the lady."

Monday 13 AUGUST

GOT into work to find the news diary depressingly empty.

Even the public relations events are pitifully dull this week.

Decided to check up on our holiday application. Delighted to hear that our request has approved by our bosses. Last day of work will be Friday this week.

SWITCHED onto the international news-wires to see if there was anything happening.

There was a report from the American Institute for Preventative Medicine which said that wearing neckties can be bad for you. They can make one's head swim and vision blur, and may have long term deleterious effects.

It sounds as if Dr Doom's theory on ties has been vindicated.

Tuesday
14
AUGUST

NEWSROOM deathly quiet. Decided to nip down to Stanley market for a long lunchbreak to pick up some holiday stuff, such as sunglasses and shorts.

In the bus depot under Exchange Square, we poised ourselves to play the Stanley Two-Step. This game consists of watching which driver emerges first from the crew quarters — the driver of bus number six (slow but cheap at HK$3.70), or the helmsman of the 260 (fast but pricey at HK$6.60).

One then scuttles to the correct bus stop.

But today, lo and behold, both drivers emerged at exactly the same time.

The queue, uncertain how to proceed, swayed unsteadily.

But what's this?

One of the drivers detoured to a mini-shrine. He extracted three joss sticks, applied the lighter, and bowed twice in solemn *bai san* fashion, which is when you bow to the shrine with joss sticks in your hands.

Then he got into the cab of bus number six.

This clear example of a driver taking out the most traditional form of Hongkong motor insurance had a definite effect on the queue, which opted, as a man, to take the number six.

ON the bus, two Australian touroids turned to ask what the business with the queue and the joss sticks had been about. We duly explained.

"Wouldn't it be safer to take the 260, which does not need the protection of prayer?" asked one.

"Wait till you see the Wongneichung Gap," we replied.

Some minutes later the bus was thundering along the perilous edge of the Gap towards Repulse Bay, with branches thumping the bus on one side, and the chasm yawning beneath the wheels on the other side.

Looked back at the touroids, who were white-faced.

They appeared to be doing their own version of *bai san.*

Wednesday 15 AUGUST

OPENED the mail to find a report about a corporate ceremony celebrated by Coca-Cola in Indonesia with a mass circumcision.

The firm decided that it would let its local agents organise a company celebration. Coca-Cola is produced in Jakarta by PT Djaya Beverages Bottling Co and PT Eska, two traditionally run firms.

They assembled a collection of small boys and a pair of sharp scissors. A total of 50 boys gave body parts in the interests of the occasion.

The centrepiece of the occasion was the moment when central Jakarta Mayor H. Abdul Munir, one of the senior invitees, ceremoniously handed over a pair of scissors to a gentleman called Dr Handarmi, who was in charge of the actual slicing-work.

We will never again complain about the boring way corporate public relations events are done in Hongkong.

LUDDITE Lo was waiting in the office when we arrived. "Have you heard the news about Japan?" he said. "They are going to change all the phone numbers in Tokyo sometime next year. It's official."

We replied that we were no longer worried about changed phone numbers.

After all, we got used to the new numbering system in Hongkong easily enough.

"That's not the point," he said. "Why do you think they are changing every single number in every major city in the world? They are re-routing calls in some way. They must be up to something. They are probably bugging them."

We replied that if it was happening to ALL the major cities, who were "they"?

"I haven't worked that out yet," he said.

CHAINSAW Charlie arrived at work in the afternoon. His cheek and mouth muscles were twitching and distorted in a strange and horrible way.

"Are you ill?" we asked.

"Never better," he said. "Have you heard the news?

"Harry Ramsden's has reconsidered its decision about expansion in the Far East.

"They are sending over several tons of fish and chips for a test run in October, and they expect a fully fledged branch to open in Hongkong next year."

So that's what a sub-editor looks like when he's smiling.

GOT to Quarry Bay to clear out our desk for the vacation.

Lo and behold, what do we find there but another bottle of scotch?

Attached was a note which said: "From your friends at the ICAC."

How baffling. Now who do we report this one to?

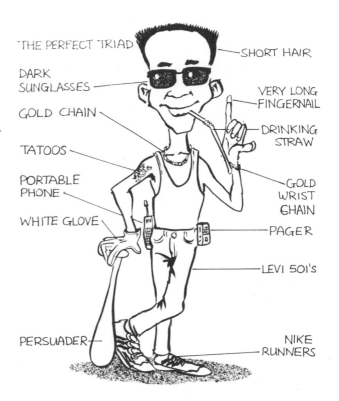

THE PERFECT TRIAD

SHORT HAIR

DARK SUNGLASSES

VERY LONG FINGERNAIL

GOLD CHAIN

DRINKING STRAW

TATOOS

PORTABLE PHONE

GOLD WRIST CHAIN

WHITE GLOVE

PAGER

LEVI 501's

PERSUADER

NIKE RUNNERS

Monday
10
SEPTEMBER

HOW worrying. Here we are back at work after a calming holiday in remote, tranquil, unspoilt Laos, and what do we find in the real world? The newpapers are full of stuff about Iraq invading Kuwait, impending war, oil price rises, world economic downturn, environmental disaster, etc.

Meanwhile, the Middle Eastern airline, Gulf Air, has just started a Hongkong advertising campaign. What great timing.

New airline staff uniforms are shown, and the headline is: "We're Flying New Colours." The same could be said of Kuwait as a whole, of course.

The ad lists the airline's destinations, including Kuwait and Baghdad.

Presumably this is targeted at Hongkong-based mercenaries, soldiers of fortune, looters, etc.

GOT a nice welcome from Chainsaw: "Hack back. Scribe in mercy dash to fill empty column."

But we couldn't believe our ears when he added: "I've just gone and looked at a car from a firm called Conned You Motors."

One of Hongkong's busiest car agents is called Conju Motors.

NOT much going on this week, except for a big property sale in Sha Tin.

The remarkable thing is that Sun Hung Kai Properties is letting people buy homes in New Town Plaza with Visa or Mastercard.

We had better add "credit card" to the list of things one should take on flat-buying missions, along with stuff needed to keep in with various groups of Hongkong triads.

These are some secret signals used in the recent past:
1. Right-hand white glove.
2. Plastic drinking straw.
3. Instant tattoo transfer kit.
4. Baseball bats.
5. False fingernail for "pinky" finger.

Property speculation is becoming complicated and expensive. Professional queuers now charge at least HK$300 for an eight-hour stint.

With queues stretching for five or six days and nights, speculation can no longer be considered a simple hobby for fun and profit.

STAFF from SHK Properties called to say they are trying out a plan to scupper organised profiteers in this week's sale.

No information will be given out about the flats until tomorrow, the day before the sale starts.

This means Mr and Mrs Average Buyer, who probably know how many children they have, have enough time to form a queue to buy a suitable flat.

But there isn't enough time for triads to organise wacky secret identification signs, such as each member wearing one galosh, carrying a stuffed albatross, etc.

MANY thanks to Gift Express Ltd for their brochure received today, offering gifts, such as bottles of fine wine, for the Mid-Autumn Festival.

But we have to report that Chainsaw took exception to your maxim: "Best to be drunk young."

"What's wrong with being an old drunk?" he demanded.

THIS fast food business is really getting out of hand.

A whole page of the *China Daily* was taken up with an announcement that the Zhejiang Meat Processing Factory in China wants to import some equipment from overseas compatriots or foreigners. The plan: put together a system to make "Bone Gruel Enriched Food".

They need: 1) some bone grinders, and 2) a bone-gruel enriched food quick freezing line.

Readers may like to check their attics/spare rooms, etc. You never know what you may find. The Zhejiang people could try Cat Street, perhaps.

THINGS were really bad on the stock market today.

Reporter Gareth Hewett called a broker and asked: "How's it going today?"

The growled reply: "Ever tried to get a f . . . at a funeral?"

"WHAT a pathetic lot stockbrokers are," said a suave-voiced caller.

"Funerals are great places to pick up girls. The best place. They are extremely sociable affairs. He should try it."

Meanwhile, brokers have been sitting around with their prospects of a Christmas bonus dwindling fast.

Vicki McGlothren of Reuters just had the following conversation with James Osborn of Baring Securities:

McGlothren: What's the market like?

Osborn: It's so quiet you can hear a salary drop.

MORE requests from the province of Zhejiang, which is apparently doing a big push on technical trade with foreign partners. They need:

1. Equipment and technology to run a "Coal Mine Chicken Farm".

2. Equipment and knowhow for "The Process of Gooseskin Furring".

3. Technology to produce "Four Billion Units of Human Chorionic Gonadotrophin".

Human gonad what? Four billion?
Does anyone know what any of this is about?

A CHAP called up today and described himself a
Hongkong-based drug dealer. He said he could
clear up the mystery about human chorionic
gonadotrophin.

This is a substance which helps small boys
with puberty problems and causes weight loss in
fatties.

"We get it from the urine of pregnant
women," he said. "They produce the heaviest
concentration between their third and fifth
month of pregnancy."

The trouble is you need huge amounts.

"It takes between 10 and 50 tons of urine to
produce one kilo of the stuff, which we usually
call HGC. But this is in a semi-crude state. When
it is fully refined, we are left with maybe 600
grammes."

China is one of the world's biggest producers
of HCG, although it seems strange that a country
with a strict birth control policy should be so.

This gentleman has the unenviable task of
visiting the factories to cement the deals. "They
are really disgusting. There are buckets and
buckets of urine all over the place," he said.

Curiously they can only make it in North
China.

"It is something to so with the unsuitable
temperature and oxygen level in south China.
The urine just goes off," he said.

How does one tell?

HOW can you get excited about the stock
market when the most dramatic quote on the
Reuters monitor report on the Hongkong share
markets says, as it did today, "Quite boring
again"?

SWITCHED on the Knight-Ridder wire and looked at the financial news.

Honest to God, this is what it said:

"Wall Street's do-nothings did it again.

"With buyers becoming an endangered species and sellers asking 'to whom', the trading temperature on the New York Stock Exchange remained as exciting as melting ice.

"Investor apathy led one broker to plead to a caller:

"'Speak to me. Nobody's calling. I just want somebody to talk to.'"

THAT oh-so-swish Joyce Ma and the gang had a meal in private rooms at the Mandarin Oriental last night, we were told by a mole who had been present.

They were celebrating the forthcoming stock market listing of mega-swanky clothes chain Joyce Boutique.

Eventually the clinking of lead crystal was interrupted by a question – an obvious one, considering the crisis now on in the Persian Gulf: "Is this really a good time for a listing?"

Ms Ma said: "God chose this time."

(The great lady is known for her spirituality.)

Our mole told us: "I didn't quite work up the courage to say: "Don't you mean Allah?"

BACK in the office, we noted that the stock markets around the region were as deadly dull as Hongkong's.

A broker in Wellington, New Zealand, contacted for a quote, told us: "It was about as exciting as kissing your sister."

What's wrong with our sister?

Saturday 22 SEPTEMBER

DIDN'T go to the office today, but Fast Buck phoned us at home to say he had just received the latest publication from the Low brothers.

They are members of a Malaysian banking family who got into trouble in Hongkong, and jumped bail to flee to Taiwan in January, 1988. From there, they write angry journals arguing their case.

"This is a really hot one," said Fast Buck. "I'll leave it in your pigeon hole at the FCC."

Monday 24 SEPTEMBER

IT WAS a hot one. The fugitive bankers have unleashed the forces of "Karmic Chaos" to descend upon their critics in Hongkong.

Lawyer Hugh Stubbs of Freshfields and Philip Bowring, editor of the *Far Eastern Economic Review,* are among the targets for this invisible 'Force of Nature".

We advise them to keep their windows closed.

Apparently this is a mystic force that descends on wrongdoers and takes vengeance.

"Karma is impartial," writes Mr Low Chung Song. "It affects all monarchs, ministers, judges and the simpletons. It works on individuals, corporations, and empires."

He seems to have left out bankers. Some we know have been having a tough time the last couple of years.

THESE new little wire-less boxes which enable you to keep in touch with financial markets are really catching on.

This is particularly true of the Hutchison Connection Box, which enables you to continuously see exactly how much money you are losing in stocks, currencies, gold, etc.

Now investors can have their day completely spoilt even when miles from a telephone.

Tuesday 25 SEPTEMBER

MY my. We *are* having a supernatural time this week.

The Barclays Bank people in Hongkong have just moved house. They lifted their eagle logo plaque from St George's Building in Central and placed it in Pacific Place, Admiralty.

Like all well-assimilated foreign firms in Hongkong, they called in a *fung shui* expert to advise them on whether they needed to install goldfish, mirrors, trees, waterfalls, crispy-fried roast piglets, etc.

This venerable mystical gentleman was just doing his stuff in the office of Barclays boss Mark Tress, when there was a flutter at the window.

A huge eagle flapped out of nowhere, settled on the ledge outside the office, a struck a pose akin to that on the Barclays logo. Explain that, skeptics.

HAVE been advised to attend a technology trade show called CeNIT tomorrow, as a possible cure for our techno-phobia. We fear it will be full of incomprehensible jargon.

We have never worked out why they call those hard little disks "floppies" and floppy bits of paper are 'hard copy'.

And computer people are supposed to be logical!

Wednesday 26 SEPTEMBER

HAD a wander around CeNIT Asia '90, the big

technology show running at the Convention Centre. Tried to read the stuff they were handing out but soon gave up. The jargon has reached a state at which it is totally incomprehensible to normal people.

Here are two actual quotes:

1) "X.400 is known by its OSI name of MOTIS (ISO 10021)".

2) "On the DEC stand, SAS under Ultrix will be shown reading Rdb tables from a VMS-based VAX, using SAS-CONNECT".

The boss of SAS, the firm extruding this second string of baffling TechSpeak is a Mr Gasper, and frankly we are not surprised.

AFTER lunch strolled around the CeNIT show again. The title of Ugliest Acronym (amid strong competition) goes to the people at stand UFO5, who call themselves IEEE.

This was exactly the sound welling up from the back of our throat.

The following comment was made by an executive leaving the show: "Someone should have been handing out T-shirts at the exit which said: "CeNIT, BiNTHERE, DuNTHAT."

We too had noticed the abominable standard of spelling in the show's title. Further evidence that Lai See's Kwik-Spel Spelling Course would be a winner.

Thursday 27 SEPTEMBER

"YOU wrote earlier this week about those Hutchison Connection Boxes that give you instant stock market information," said a voice on the phone.

"Well I take a minibus every day, which hurtles along Conduit Road at about 130 kms an hour. This afternoon he did the whole journey with one hand on his Connection Box," he said.

Driving with one hand is dangerous, we said.

"One knee you mean. His other hand was on a Jockey Club remote terminal."

So the driver would have seen how the stock market plummeted all day today?

"Yes. And the news did nothing to improve his driving," he said.

PICKED up the *Hongkong Government Gazette Supplement Number Six,* and read a bit titled: "Application for a liquor licence to be considered by the regional council liquor licencing board in October."

The application was from the Hei Ling Chau Addiction Treatment Centre.

Come off it, chaps. You're putting temptation in your path.

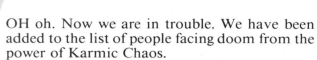

OH oh. Now we are in trouble. We have been added to the list of people facing doom from the power of Karmic Chaos.

"Please don't joke about Karmic Chaos," said the letter we received today from Mr Low, the fugitive banker from Taiwan.

"You learn best when misfortune struck and you are at your own deathbed."

Oh dear. This is rather worrying. Mr Low may not fancy coming back to face the music. But the force of Karmic Chaos is not subject to immigration department control.

ONE of our colleagues, Sondra Wudunn, returned from Japan today with some news of a dangerous-sounding product: those fiendishly brilliant Japanese have come up with the ultimate torture device for the 1990s — the Karaoke Koach.

This is a tour bus with karaoke screens embedded in the ceiling and microphones with extra long leads, so that they can be passed around the seats, enabling each passenger to contribute to the, er, entertainment (isn't that what they call it?).

Just like in a real karaoke lounge, the bus is lit by fake crystal chandeliers.

"We were on it for hours. All the songs were in Japanese," said Sondra, still traumatised by the experience.

Lai See demands to know: how much do drivers of Karaoke Koaches get paid?

Whatever it is, it is not enough.

IN the evening, we dined at the Hongkong Club, which serves possibly the best club food in Hongkong. We got talking about the karaoke disease to a local businessman who frequently visits Japan on business.

He said: "One thing has always baffled me about it. You go out with a bunch of Japanese businessmen and they always sing the same song: *My Way*. But if you understand how Japanese businesses are structured, the staff never do it their way. They do it the boss's way. They should be clutching a picture of Akio Morita and singing *I Did It His Way*."

IS there a monster lurking in the dark waters of Chek Lap Kok, the tranquil bay on Lantau island that may one day be Hongkong International Airport?

We ask after visiting this idyllic spot in a junk at the weekend.

The sea was strangely turbulent. And there were shoals of silvery flying fish that kept leaping out of the water as if being chased.

Skipper Noel Rands, a banker from Midland Montagu in Hongkong, was down in the galley dishing up curry when the rest of the party saw a glimpse of a much larger aquatic creature break the surface.

Could it be a distant relative of the Loch Ness Monster? Those would-be airport-builders may get a rude shock!

SOMETHING large has definitely been spotted swimming off the coast of northern Lantau, we heard today from a number of callers. (In addition to Mr Rands.)

It seems to be indigenous to the area around Chek Lap Kok, Sha Chau and Black Point. Not many yuppie-junks head out that way, but the few which do have spotted it.

The Kok Ness Monster differs from his Scottish cousin. It has pink flesh, and the longest one seen so far has been 12 feet long, according to witnesses.

You don't think they could have started some sort of nuclear activity in Lantau without telling people who go swimming there, do you?

We know two advertising chaps who regularly go skinny-dipping there, and we haven't seen them for ages.

THE Business Post secretary showed us a blouse she had bought from Stanley Market on Sunday. It looked like a real "designer" piece, but after examining the label we decided it was a fake.

Look closely and you realise it doesn't say "Louis Feraud."

It says: "Louise Fraud."

THE large pink things in Kok Ness are not mutant swimmers, we were relieved to hear today, but probably Pearl River Dolphins.

Ms Meg Corrick, who works for finance firm

GT Management, has frequently seen this rare species of pinky-white dolphin from her coastal home not far from Tuen Mun. "I can see them from my living room," she said.

But this doesn't mean there is no monster. She once saw the back of a big black creature rise from the water and then disappear — and the visible bit alone was 12 feet long.

"We didn't see the whole thing, because it didn't come right out of the water," she said. "We thought it may have been a whale. But that may be the monster."

PEOPLE in the Hongkong Club that night were talking about Dr Doom's new job.

It seems that the moneyman is now working on the side as an importer of beer.

We think they said it was called Grolsch. But most words come out like that when you have drunk as much as they had.

CLUB Volvo is changing its name to Club Nova, we hear from a source whose identity will be concealed to protect him from his large and dangerous wife.

Our suggestions of Club Ovlov and Club Vulva have been scorned.

Unfortunately "Nova" means "no go" in Spanish.

THE Hongkong stockmarket is in a nervous state today. Mr Deng Xiaoping has not been seen for ages, and a stockbroker from Citicorp Scrimgeour Vickers told us he has been conspicuously absent from the Asian Games, which have been held in Beijing.

"He would normally be expected to have dominated the proceedings," he said.

We know he is sprightly, but did they really expect him to do all that running and jumping?

THINGS on the Tokyo stock market must be really bad. We bumped into Dr Doom at the Foreign Correspondents' Club sipping Grolsch at lunchtime.

He had been selling his "puts" he had on the Nikkei Index.

Does this mean that he has turned bullish?

"Certainly not. I only sold SOME of them," he replied, clearly affronted.

BACK at the office we mentioned to Chainsaw that anyone who had followed Marc Faber's tip at the start of this year to sell Japan short would have seen their investment multiplied by 20 by now.

"Hopefully that will compensate for the way he predicted disaster throughout the bull run," scoffed Chainsaw.

CHINA has well and truly discovered the power of advertising, we read in our *China Daily* this morning.

There are now 557 advertising agencies in Shanghai alone.

The most successful slogan has been for Nestle coffee: "It tastes good."

"This has become so familiar to local people that even pre-school children can recite it just for fun," reports the *China Daily*.

We can just picture them reciting it for fun.

"It tastes good."

"Oh what fun! Say it again, Comrade!"

"It tastes good."

(Children fall over, overcome with fun.)

Tuesday 9 OCTOBER

CHINA correspondent Geoff Crothall reported that the best known ad campaign in Shanghai at the moment is for Baili Beauty Soap, which allegedly makes users younger. The slogan is: "Twenty years old this year — and 18 years old next year."

Perhaps Mr Deng has locked himself away with some Baili Beauty Soap?

DR Doom told us that he has no plans to give up the money side completely and turn beer baron.

"I did look at the figures and found that you need to sell an awful lot of beer to make any decent sort of money at all," he said.

But the beer tastes good, and since his wife is involved in the food and drink business it seemed a natural step.

We promised the money doctor that we would try and think up a slogan for him.

BACK at the office, Chainsaw had a good idea for a marketing angle for Dr Doom's new beer.

"Grolsch is the only beer you can still pronounce after drinking 10 pints," he said. "Imagine saying 'Czechoslovakian Pilsener Urquell' after a heavy session. 'Chek Pilsh . . . er, Shek Bilge . . . Er, gimme a Grolsch.'"

Wednesday 10 OCTOBER

WE hear that the dreamers of Hollywood are thinking of making a film of *Chung Kuo*, the futuristic novel set in China.

The US film makers are in the pre-production stage, and are trying to decide who should take the role of Hans Ebert. On the list is Mel Gibson, the hunky Australian star.

"The trouble is, I don't think we look alike at

all," the hirsute **Mr Ebert** told us.

"Perhaps if they had hired Cat Stevens before he went off to become an enemy of Salman Rushdie . . . ?"

WE note that the proponents of advertising in China are learning all the tricks of their counterparts in freer markets.

Or so we deduce after today seeing an advertisement for Anhui Fresh Eggs, produced by the snappily-named China National Cereals Oils and Foodstuffs Import and Export Corp Anhui Branch.

It features a photograph of three eggs, overlaid with three sentences:

"EGGS which are a natural phenomenon.

"Produced by hens individually.

"Packaged: ie, each one is in a self-contained shell."

Perhaps they need to do some more work on the "Unique selling proposition" concept.

We wonder what they think eggs from elsewhere are like?

Thursday 11 OCTOBER

CONVERSATION at 9.55 am yesterday with secretary to a Manulife insurance consultant:

Caller: Hello, is Don Fearon there?

Secretary: No. He has gone to lunch.

That even beats our personal record.

THE following incident took place today.

The scene: an exhibition of original 19th and 20th century British paintings, in the Malaysia Room of the Hongkong Hilton.

Two bankers stop near a painting labelled as being by the great colonial painter George Chinnery.

First banker: That's rather nice. Shall we buy it?

Second banker: No thanks. We have already got it.

(Moment of silence.)

Then they realised that both the paintings mentioned in their brief discussion were aliegedly "the original".

The one the first banker was talking about was in the vaults of the Hongkong Bank, as part of the bank's huge art collection.

The other painting, also "the original," was for sale to any passing tycoon.

A typical scene in Hongkong's flourishing arts and antiques business.

Friday
12
OCTOBER

WE were nipping through the electronics fair at the convention centre in Wan Chai today when we came upon an unusual invitation in the shape of a sign outside a stall full of computer monitors.

"Come In and Test Our VD Transmissions For Yourself," it said.

This seemed outrageously suggestive.

Have they discovered that computer screens cause even more problems for people than originally believed?

BACK in the office on a languorous Friday afternoon, we were pleased to find proof that the advertising industry in China is coming along by leaps and bounds.

China-watcher Simon Clennell showed us an advertisement for 101 hair Regrowth Linament in the *China Daily*.

There are two photographs, captioned "Before" and "After".

The "Before" picture shows a man with a full head of hair. The "After" picture shows a man with almost no hair. Clearly a case of truth-in-advertising taken to its limits.

Monday 15 OCTOBER

MUCH gloom in the backrooms of the Hongkong Bank headquarters, we hear, where they have been trying to organise Trailwalker, an all-day-and-all-night walk of 100 kms to raise money for charity.

Each year, the cash target has been raised, and last year 400 teams raised a record HK$2.5 million.

But this year it is going to be different. Because of the economic downturn, the target will not be raised. "It may even be lowered," one of the organisers revealed to us.

Men and Women in Dark Suits are generally not keen to give away large amounts of their own cash during economic downturns, she said.

Or indeed at any other times.

Tuesday 16 OCTOBER

"LOWER the target? Nonsense! We'll do the first two mill by ourselves!"

Who made this amazing declaration? Four of the Hongkong business community's most high-profile Suits.

They plan to raise HK$2 million by themselves and thus personally guarantee that the Trailwalker target will be overshot.

Our headline writer immediately named the team The Million Dollar Men.

They are: Paul Selway-Swift, general manager of the Hongkong Bank, Simon Murray, taipan of Hutchison Whampoa, Martin Spurrier, boss of the Rowland Co and John Gatehouse, boss of Warburg Asset Management.

Even their back-up driver is a big name in business. The support man (the chap with the van-full of snacks and clean socks) will be Willy Fung, boss of Li and Fung, the Toys 'R' Us people in Hongkong.

This we've got to see.

A WAVE of social awareness is sweeping over the Dark Suit Brigade.

Large numbers of them are clamouring to join Trailwalker — not just by giving money, but by actually doing the 100 km walk.

Thirty-eight teams from banks have signed on, with 22 teams from The Bank alone. Accountants and lawyers are neck-and-neck in the charitableness stakes, with 16 teams of each having made the pledge to suffer 30 to 40 hours of agony.

Even Ted Thomas, the not-a-spring-chicken PR man, is going to tramp over the hills all day and all night.

This is frankly bizarre.

What will happen to the Hongkong business community's hard-won reputation for being sternly single-minded in their pursuit of Mammon?

WE have been enjoying reading *Target* magazine recently.

A gentleman by the name of Marc Hitchen has, for some months, been enthusiastically throwing himself into his job there. His patch: writing about fraud.

"Company fraud and related naughtinesses — all the juicy bits," he told us.

Nice to see someone who really enjoys his work.

A RUMOUR is running around Exchange Square that several Suits plan to be "in a meeting" during Trailwalker and delegate the 100 km walk to their personal assistants.

Surely this cannot be true?

THERE has been some strange nudging and winking at the FCC bar about Marc Hitchen, the charming gentleman who writes about fraud matters at *Target.* What can this mean?

Friday 19 OCTOBER

THE scene: a preparatory meeting for teams taking part in Trailwalker. The cast: a lot of mere mortals, and, nestled inconspicuously among them, The Million Dollar Men.

The organisers started by warning that a dim view would be taken of anyone who called for the official rescue helicopter because they had a headache or sore feet.

But they did not say anything about contestants who could afford to bring their own helicopters, so Our Boys are all right there.

People can bed down for a nap in a tent but no one is allowed to check into any hotels en route, said the organisers.

There was some quick rustling of maps. The only inns near the route were the infamous Kowloon Tong "love hotels". The Million Dollar Men would not be seen dead near them, for their reputations' sakes, so that temptation was definitely out.

Organiser Maggie Brook then said she had heard that the best diet for walkers was cold rice pudding, fruit cake and Coca-Cola left out until it had gone flat.

The Million Dollar Men, used to the finest of foodstuffs, gamely resisted the urge to flinch.

But all of a sudden, one whispered to us later, HK$2 million seemed barely enough.

Saturday 20 OCTOBER

WE heard the strangest tale about Marc Hitchen,

the fraud writer at *Target* magazine today.

Apparently he had been involved in a property company in the UK which came to an abrupt end.

The result: officers from fraud investigation bodies in that country suddenly became interested in chatting to him.

FINALLY caught up with Mr Hitchen and mentioned this to him.

"Ah, so you've heard about that?" he said. "The bit about fraud and the property business in the UK is sadly true. It was following that unfortunate business that I, er, fled to the South China Seas."

His "close-up" knowledge of company fraud could arguably be seen as making him the perfect man for the job of writing about it, he suggested hopefully.

But no. It was not to be.

Now that the news was out, he was out of a job. Mr Hitchen said he made his last visit to the Wan Chai offices of *Target* magazine on Saturday.

"I did think about handing in my resignation in the form of a story, but decided not to," he said. "There's too much irony in it."

AMAZED by a story on the newswires about a woman in the Philippines giving birth to a mudfish, which she had named Angelina.

Apparently the semi-aquatic creature spoke, saying: "Ik-ik-ik." The parents don't know what this means.

No research has ever been done on mudfish languages, largely because mudfish don't have voices.

In our opinion, this is conclusive proof that nuclear reactors should not be built in Daya Bay.

Tuesday 23 OCTOBER

A PUBLISHING man in Hongkong showed us a letter he has just received from Credit Agricole in France. It was addressed to "Hongkong, Great Britain".

Geographically the finance firm is a bit out, but politically it has an interesting point.

THE Ninja Turtles film man, Russell Cawthorne, was looking terribly cheery at the bar at lunchtime.

He has just had a remarkable letter. It asks whether he is available to be a delegate-guest at a conference in Hawaii. Air tickets, first class hotel accommodation and everything else will be thrown in, gratis.

The organisers ask whether he will be able to stay on an extra week, to tour the islands for pleasure.

"Well, it is a rotten job but someone has to do it," he mused, already mentally enjoying the hulahula dancing on the beach.

Wednesday 24 OCTOBER

QUIET day at work, so had a long lunch. Found Russell Cawthorne back at the bar, but not looking nearly as happy as he was yesterday.

He had made inquiries about his free trip to Hawaii.

Apparently he was supposed to have replied by October 10 to qualify for it.

But the letter went astray (someone in the post office business thought Hongkong was in the Philippines), and arrived much too late for him to accept.

No wonder his face was the sickly green colour

of those turtles he is always on about.

CHINA'S first grain market has just opened for business, we heard from Geoff Crothall in China.

On hand at the opening of the market in Zhengzhou, Henan Province, was Mr William Grossman, vice-president of the world's biggest futures market, the Chicago Board of Trade.

This is exciting news. China produces a huge amount of grain, and yet, up to now, has had little ability to sell it in the world's commodity markets.

This could indicate a prosperous future for the whole region.

"DON'T get too excited," said stockbroker Big Swinging Richard, a large gentleman with a pendulous lovelife, over lunch at Brown's Wine Bar.

"To be precise, the Chinese market is almost, but not quite, a futures market. It should technically be called a 'forward market'," he explained.

This is because if you buy a HK$500,000 soyabean contract, you actually have to arrange transport and take delivery of commodities ordered."

The first transaction was for 4,500 tons of wheat flour.

We hope the broker knows what he is doing or has a BIG spare room.

THE dodgy practice of sticking on a surcharge for paying by plastic has spread to St Paul's Hospital in Causeway Bay.

A friend of ours sadly ended up in need of treatment there shortly after he had proudly acquired his first American Express card. We don't think there was any direct connection between the two events.

But when he thrust his card at the hospital cash desk to pay his bill, he was informed they wanted an extra 3.5 per cent.

We expect dodgy little camera shops in Tsim Sha Tsui to get up to these tricks.

But a hospital?

INTRIGUED by the vivid blue envelope on our desk today.

"Dear Reader," it said. "Keeping up to date with what is happening in the International Financial World and more importantly how your investment portfolio is performing can be a time-consuming exercise."

If we fill in a questionnaire, we get free gifts, including "a discounted offer to attend the Hongkong Money Show, Asia's leading investment exhibition."

The Money Show was three weeks ago.

It just goes to show.

Keeping up to date with what is happening in the international financial world can be a time-consuming exercise, as we read somewhere recently.

THIS is a real life conversation that took place yesterday.

Caller: Can I please speak to the managing director?

Receptionist: Hello.

Caller: Can I please speak to the managing director?
Receptionist: How to spell?
Caller: Can I PLEASE speak to the managing director?
Receptionist: What is your name?
Caller: Mr Smith.
Receptionist: Mr Smith is not in.
Click.

MR Bob Howlett, managing editor of *Hongkong,inc,* told us that his children, based in Adelaide, Australia, had just visited him in the territory.

"They told me that they had a new sex education teacher," he said.

"The old one was called Mrs Horne. The new one is called Mrs Safe."

Talk about a sign of the times.

THEY say that driving your body too hard can cause hallucinations.

This evening, Million Dollar Man Simon Murray was on the first leg of Trailwalker.

As he approached the Sai Sha Road checkpoint, after 30 foot-blistering kilometres of difficult trekking, he came upon a bizarre sight.

Slick PR supremo Ted Thomas had got there ahead of him, and was casually presiding over a dinner table laid for eight.

"You on this too?" asked muscled ex-Legionnaire Murray incredulously, recalling

Thomas's penchant for extensive lunches at the Hongkong Club.

"Yep," replied the laconic PR man, tucking into fettucine alfredo and taking a large draught of Gevrey Chambertin burgundy from a silver chalice.

SEVERAL jet-black hours later, the first rays of dawn appeared. Mr Murray and the rest of The Million Dollar Men reached Beacon Hill, 60 agony-filled kilometres from the start.

But lo! There was Thomas, leaning back in his chair at an impeccably laid breakfast table of sausages, eggs and bacon, sizzled on a row of primus stoves. Behind him a set of bedding and tents was being packed away.

"How's it going, Ted?" asked footsore banker Paul Selway-Swift, marvelling at the Christofle tableware.

Ted nodded his greetings, his mouth stopped by eggs benedict.

AT lunchtime, at Lead Mine Pass, after a bone-chilling downpour, walkers came upon the omnipresent Thomas ladling soup into Crown Derby chinaware.

What's going on?

How can Ted get so far ahead of these super-fit heroes that he can stop and cook gourmet meals?

Something fishy going on.

"TED was not walking," said a voice on the phone. "He decided at the last minute that he'd be more useful in a, er, back-up role."

He was supporting two teams, one called

Corporate Communications Girls (Melanie Hunt, Miranda Shiel, Edward Lupton and David Shiel) and one called Masonic School Old Girls (Ted's wife Nicola Parkinson, sister Arabella, their papa Duncan and a family friend Annette Don).

The cynical mole on Thomas's staff added: "Huh. He just wanted to make sure we would be all right to be in the office on time on Monday morning. The firm bills clients for staff work done by the hour, you see."

Monday 5 NOVEMBER

AT least there is one place where fast food does not dominate the scene.

The cabbages arrived in Beijing today, we heard from Mr Crothall.

Truckloads of them. People were seen wheeling away precarious mountains of cabbages in wheelbarrows and baby carriages.

Last year the authorities grew several million cabbages too many and ended up ordering work units to buy the rotting vegetables.

This year, the authorities have grown 8,200 hectares instead of 9,400 hectares, according to the Chief Manager – Vegetables at the Beijing Agriculture Bureau.

"Young people may have lost their taste for cabbages," reported the *China Daily*. "But the old Beijingers feel unprepared for the season if they do not have 200 to 300 kg stored in their courtyards or balconies."

Suddenly, a Big Mac seems almost delectable.

WHAT a furore followed the little piece we printed on St Paul's Hospital demanding surcharges from patients who paid with plastic money.

We have had lots of calls, and the matter was discussed at length on Ralph Pixton's Open Line on the radio. Must remember to call the chap in the hospital tomorrow. We hope he has not met with any further accidents.

Tuesday 6 NOVEMBER

THE patient concerned in the St Paul's Hospital surcharge dispute returned to the hospital in Causeway Bay to settle his debt, we found out this morning.

He went to the payment desk and specifically asked whether the improper 3.5 per cent surcharge remained on his bill.

Staff proudly assured him it was no longer present.

Then one staffer explained that they had neatly hidden the charge by incorporating it into other charges on the bill.

Of course he blew his top and refused to pay it.

In the end, this fellow was sitting on the desk in a fury. Staff, including nuns in habits, were running around him saying things like: "Really, we have no desire to cheat anyone."

We feel sure that the nuns are not trying to con patients.

But they really don't seem to understand how plastic money works.

Wednesday 7 NOVEMBER

WE are getting some very strange reports on the foreign exchange wires.

Citibank Australia's Forex Forwards Commentary claims Angelina the Mudfish is still alive. The Holy Mudfish of the Philippines is secretly being groomed to lead a normal life.

"All was well until a recent incident where her guardians took her to McDonald's," revealed Citibank.

One of the party thoughtlessly ordered a Filet O' Fish, and Angelina suffered a nervous breakdown after seeing one of her brethren smothered in mayonnaise inside a sesame bun. Is Citibank sending coded signals?

ANOTHER bulletin on the forex wire about Angelina. She has now decided to go for a modelling career and has been spotted calling up a magazine and saying: "Ik-ik-ik."

We can only imagine that this is some deep metaphor for the bizarre recent behaviour of the Australian dollar, which yesterday rose tantalisingly to 99.99 yen.

GOT a call from one of Hongkong's biggest "headhunting" firms — you know, the people who spot talented individuals and offer them high-paid jobs as CEOs etc.

He said: "Could we have lunch together sometime? I want to talk to you about something."

We understand that this is normal headhunter code that precedes the offer of a job.

Chainsaw however very skeptical about the whole thing.

EAGERLY tuned into the FX Forwards Commentary to hear the latest on Angelina the Mudfish.

But there was no news — only a message that there may not be any more.

She is getting too much coverage, according to the forex office at Citibank Australia.

"We wouldn't want her to become Angelina

Minogue," said the message.

DECIDED to put a certain sub-editor in his place. We called the headhunter and asked bluntly what this planned lunch was all about.

"I've been promoted," he said. "I thought you might be able to get my photograph into the new appointments column in the newspaper."

ON a weekend visit to the Oriental in Singapore, the Mandarin Oriental group hotel in that fine city-state, we received the following message:
"Dear Sir,
"Please collect your air ticket from the concierge desk upon your departure today.
"Thank you.
"Mustaffa Concierge."
Talk about an appropriate name. After all, every hotel mustaffa concierge.

HAVE arranged to see another headhunter, Mr Peter Roberts of MSL, on Monday next week to pick up some information about how they are coping with the present bizarre situation, ie. the brain drain, labour shortage, negative unemployment rate, etc.

POPPED in to see the wonderful Jockey Club exhibition The Year of the Horse, in the underbelly of the Hongkong Bank HQ.
This has some remarkable educational exhib-

its. We had never seen a pile of horse laxatives before.

There are photographs of the air-conditioned living quarters of the horses, and a picture of a horse having a swim in the cool blue waters of their "equines only" circular indoor pool.

Chainsaw remarked that parts of the exhibition were as interesting as watching the grass grow.

We thought this was rather a rude comment, even by his standards.

Until we turned the corner and saw what he meant. There is a section on how grass grows. This is illustrated with a series of photographs of areas of grass, with captions such as :

"One week later.

"Another two weeks later.

"About three weeks later."

ONE of the most common questions we are asked is: why did the Lai See column change from being all about stock market tips to being gossip about Hongkong people generally?

It is because there is an insularity about stockbrokers in Hongkong which makes brokers' gossip unsuitable for general publication.

For example, one of the conversations we had this morning was absolutely typical of the sort of calls we get.

Broker: Is that Lai See? Ha ha ha. I've got the perfect story for you. You'll absolutely LOVE this one. Got a pen? Ha ha ha.

Lai See: Yes, go ahead.

Broker: Just write this down. "A little bird told me today that a certain Hongkong stockbroker nicknamed Big Boy had a funny incident happen to him on the way home from the bar at 3 am this morning. Ha ha ha. He keeps getting embarrassed whenever anyone comes up to him and says the words: 'What about last night, then, John?'" Ha ha ha."

Lai See: Go on.

Broker: That's it.

Lai See: But what does it mean?

Broker: It's an in-joke. Everybody will find it really funny.

Lai See: Everybody?

Broker: Everybody in our office.

This is a genuine example of the kind of thing we have to put up with virtually every day.

ONE of the great mysteries of the Hongkong business scene has been solved by our mysterious banking contact, Mr Soixante-Neuf.

Why do Hongkong business people always stand on street corners having conversations on their mobile phones?

"That way the tips they get cannot be classified as inside information," he said.

DREAMS of achieving Yuptopia are over for one individual.

We don't know why, but he has been advertising what is more or less a complete check-list of Essential Artifacts for the Hongkong Yuppie.

"Hutchison Mobile Phone, 10 months old, (HK$14,000). Movado and Bulova his/hers watches (HK$1,500 and HK$650). Leather deskset (HK$600). Technics synthesizer tuner (HK$800). Porsche pilot case and briefcase (HK$7,000 and HK$5,000). New Cartier wallet (HK$700)."

We cannot help but wonder why someone should give up yuppiehood in so wholesale a fashion. Has he renounced materialism?

What is Hongkong coming to?

THEY are extremely strict at the Grand Hyatt's Champagne Bar.

Once the few seats are filled, that's it.

No one else is allowed in.

We were ejected from the bar tonight for daring to suggest that there was plenty of room for thirsty people to guzzle champers (at HK$98 a glass) while standing up.

TEE hee. We hear that a certain distinguished looking foreign gentleman had the same experience at the Grand Hyatt's Champagne Bar this evening as we had last night.

He was stopped at the door, told about the no standing rule, and firmly turned away.

You know who he was?

Only the organiser of the Hongkong Forex Conference — a chap who has directly and indirectly just spent millions of dollars at the hotel. Most of the delegates stayed there.

We are delighted to see that the same rules apply to all classes of champagne quaffers.

But we hope the cashiers will understand if he settles his bill in Albanian Leks and Matatutse Gumbo Beans.

CONVERSATION between our Discovery Bay mole and residents' club staff on this evening.

Mole: Can you put me through to the restaurant please?

Staff: Yes, sir.

Mole: Is that the restaurant?

Staff: Yes, sir.

Mole: Can I book a table for two at 7.45 pm?

Staff: Would you like the Western restaurant

or the Chinese restaurant?
    Mole: Which is available?
    Staff: They are both full.

THE toughest thing about being a headhunter is keeping a straight face during interviews, we learned from Peter Roberts of MSL Pacific today. "You'd be amazed at what people say," he said.

It must be the stress of Hongkong life. Here are some recent quotes:

● "When the interviewer asked me what my weaknesses are, I later realised that 'smoking and eating chocolate' was not the answer he was seeking."

● "I am looking for a new job because my boss does not want me living with my girlfriend."

● "No, I am not working at the moment. I'm having my lunch hour."

● "I understood your company was a massage parlour."

● "Do you mind if I take my shoes off while you interview me?"

● "I suppose I really got the hint that my boss wanted me to leave when he told me I had a body odour problem."

● "I'm sorry I'm late but my skirt got ripped off in the lift."

Perhaps the saddest quote came from a chap who wanted his interviewers to think he was in great demand.

● "People are after me. Following my recent job application, I got down to the last 25."

AN even more disastrous job interview tale arrived today from the files of Search and Assessment

Services. This chap arrived for his interview and was told by a woman that the managing director had been called away but she would talk to him instead.

Assuming she was an assistant or secretary, he made an awful fuss. Fie! He did not wish to be interviewed by a secretary.

She turned out to be the chairwoman of the board of directors, in other words, the boss's boss's boss.

He didn't get the job.

What are we to make of this announcement?

Goldcorp's Hongkong office is to make changes to the Kangaroo Nugget gold coin. It now features a red kangaroo. This will be replaced with a grey kangaroo, it says.

Unfortunately, the coins are not in colour.

SENIOR tax manager Andrew Yates of Deloitte Haskins and Sells got an eye-catching offer in the mail.

"Projecting Your Image As A Successful Woman" was the title of the HK$1,850 seminar to which he was being invited at the Excelsior hotel.

At the workshop, he would receive "the woman manager's survival kit". He would learn how to make the most of his "feminine talents". He would learn how to cope with those "sticky situations" in which business women find themselves.

We imagine one definition of a sticky situation is for women executives to accidentally send invitations like this to men.

Friday
23
NOVEMBER

NEEDED a treat, so we ordered "scones with jam and cream" in the Lane Crawford coffee shop on the fifth floor of their Queen's Road main shop.

But only one of the delectable yummies appeared as part of the HK$44 tea set.

We remonstrated strongly that the word "scones" indicated the presence of more than one.

The result: spirited debate involving staff and manageress as to whether "scones" indicated plurality.

Eventually it was agreed that it did and a second one was brought.

People are always complaining about the standard of English in Hongkong, but what about the maths?

Monday
26
NOVEMBER

STOCK market booms always appear where you least expect them, said Big Swinging Richard.

"That's why people haven't noticed where the latest one is," he added, and then paused for effect. "China. Shenzhen."

There are only five companies listed in Shenzhen, he said. One has gone up 16-fold since being listed in March, and another has risen 70-fold since May 1987.

We asked him how investors can get their money into the Shenzhen market.

"You can't," he said. "That's the downside."

He can be annoyingly unpractical at times.

But he did offer to introduce us to a chap from the mainland tomorrow who knows all about the Shenzhen stock market.

WE heard a story today that reveals just how

polluted Hongkong is. Builders here have ordered more than 120 kilometres of wrapping tape from Arnhold and Co. The tape will be used in Hongkong's Effluent Export Scheme, a plan to send millions of gallons of sewage far out into the sea through a giant pipe.

One would assume the tape would be needed to keep the obnoxious substances in the pipe.

But no. The tape is needed to protect the pipe and its contents (sewage) from the soil.

Tuesday 27 NOVEMBER

THE name of this sewage plan got us thinking.

Is sewage which goes out through the Effluent Export Scheme counted by the Census and Statistics Department as Domestic Exports?

If so, what about the sewage that comes from tourist hotels, filled with foreigners? Surely, that should go down in the trade books as Re-Exports?

Also, this tape: is it the longest toilet roll in the world? Shouldn't someone tell *The Guinness Book of Records?*

Yes, another important number one for Hongkong.

"THE baby stock market in Shenzhen is having an effect on the rest of China," we were told by Swinging Richard's friend.

When Shenzhen, the capitalistic special economic zone, first started to get richer than its neighbours, there was an outflow of cash to the rest of China.

But now, for the first time, there is an inflow of money to Shenzhen.

People are pulling out thousands of crumpled renminbi notes from their mattresses and posting them to Shenzhen, so their Third Nephews and Fourth Uncles can put them on the stock market.

"YOU think passions run high among the daredevil players in the Hongkong share market? You should see the punters in Shenzhen."

This was from Swinging Richard over hairy crab at the Great Shanghai Restaurant in Prat Avenue.

A pair of best friends got into the investing game on the fledgling Shenzhen stock market, and then fell out over the winnings from their share transactions.

"They eventually shot each other dead," he said.

The gunfight failed to halt the momentum, and prices continued to soar.

Communism just isn't what it used to be.

BY the way, researcher Five-Finger Wu finally seems to have discovered the ultimate Chinese medical product: a cure for cancer, available in bottles.

China No 1 Tian Xian Liquid, imported by the China-Japan Fedia Medicine Co of Chatham Road, Tsim Sha Tsui has "a success rate of 80.7 per cent on cancer patients in the middle or late stages of the disease".

It received two major awards in the 38th World Eureka Invention Expo:

1. World's Best Individual Invention.

2. Medal of Honour from the King of Belgium.

We were impressed enough by the title of World's Best Individual Invention. But a Medal of Honour from the King of Belgium? What greater accolade can any product get?

WHAT are we to make of the offer of one million

condoms being offered by an advertisement in a Hongkong publication this week?

The price is a mere HK$180,000, which makes them 18 cents each.

The stock is largely made up of "3,660 gross of Loose Condom," it says.

Is this just an incredibly badly chosen brand name?

Or are they cheap because they have problems fitting? If so, we don't think the buyer need worry. Can you imagine any male returning a condom and complaining that it is too big?

It just wouldn't happen.

WE were crossing the walkway to Exchange Square when we came across a large number of youths handing out leaflets from the Hongkong European Tailoring Factory.

This is a Causeway Bay suitmaker which has been involved in many legal wrangles. It promises delivery by certain dates, but has a strange sense of time.

The leaflet says: "You can ask this boys or girls to take you to our Factory. Only take five minutes by walking or 15 minutes by taxi."

LAI See has just had a letter from Arnold King, president of the grand-sounding World Public Relations Centre in Nathan Road, Tsim Sha Tsui.

"Dear Sir/Madam,

"The third time of PR Conference which is organised by us will be held in Manila, Philippines on March 20-23, 1991, the secretariat of this conference will welcome you warmly for your attending to discuss freely with other counterparts. People have discovered using PR to smooth the situations, solve the problems, to link the bridge between consumers and suppliers and ease the crisis and conflicts among nations. With regard to recent Gulf crisis PR can abolish to burst out with great possibilities."

We realise Mr King's heart is in the right place, but personally we would be happier if he did not try to use his PR communication skills to end the Middle-East war situation.

Something may burst out with great possibilities.

WE sneaked back into Lane Crawford, the top people's shop, this week, to find that they have gone back to serving one scone at a time.

The 's' has been Tipp-exed off the word 'scones' on every menu.

AT the FCC tonight, several people were talking
about the *Asiaweek* Christmas party coming up
at the Hilton ballroom on Monday.

This has become a ritual in which large
numbers of arch-rivals in the Hongkong
publishing world get together and drink gin.

The grandeur of the event, which few small
Hongkong publishing groups could afford,
seems to hypnotise mortal enemies into
behaving themselves.

"There will be a large number of axes being
buried at the party," we said.

"In the ground or in people's heads?" asked

Bretigne Shaffer from *Executive* magazine.

Yes, that's the sort of party it is likely to be.

SIPPING G. and T. at the *Asiaweek* party, Joan Howley, publisher of *Asian Finance*, attempted to disagree.

"Actually, Hongkong publishers are a friendly lot, and we all feel sorry when one of us goes under," she said.

Then her smile changed angle and her voice changed key. "With a few exceptions," she added, eyeing a rival publisher inhaling a two-kilo guacamole dip nearby.

Meanwhile, who was that in the other corner scoffing samosas?

None other than Mr Ken McKenzie, chief of *Media* magazine. This was pretty remarkable. *Asiaweek* is involved in litigation with *Media* magazine.

Berton Woodward, a senior *Asiaweek* executive, said that their annual get-togethers had a tradition of bringing together warring guests.

"At our tenth birthday party in Manila in 1985, we had Imelda Marcos and Cory Aquino," he said.

The ladies weren't big pals at the time.

AT Stanley's Oriental, we met voracious writer and feeder Kevin Sinclair. He had just read a news report about a Vietnamese woman in Hongkong who claims that she deserves refugee status because she comes from a devout Roman Catholic family and her grandfather was a priest.

"Her grandfather?" commented Kevin.

CRIMINALS in Hongkong are a zany bunch. So says polytechnic lecturer Robin Bradbeer, who visited Mark-Up and Spencer in Pacific Place to look for a pair of shoes.

That shop puts both shoes of a pair on the rack, unlike most Hongkong shoe shops where they put only the left or the right.

Anyway, as he was looking along the row, he noticed a pair that was slightly different to the others. Close examination revealed that they were in fact an old and worn pair.

Clearly, somebody had just been in, tried on a pair, found them to his liking and walked off in them.

Possibly it was the Christmas spirit that prompted the thief to recall that giving is as important as receiving, thus inspiring him to donate his old shoes to the store.

"I've heard the expression about things 'walking' from shops but have never thought of it literally," said Robin.

Wednesday
5
DECEMBER

"WHAT is the legal position on shoe thefts at Mark-Up and Spencer?" we asked a contact of ours called the Legal Beagle.

"It has some interesting possibilities," said the Beagle. "Does the fact that the thief has made a gift of a pair of shoes to Mark-Up and Spencer count as payment in kind?"

"Could an accused thief make a counter-claim against Mark-Up and Spencer, which clearly has a pair of his shoes in their possession?"

WE were pleased to get a Christmas card from the sage Ian MacFarlane of Wardley Investment Services today.

Merry Christmas to you too, Ian.

But why is there a yellow stick-on note inside, in your secretary's handwriting, saying: "Please sign." Do you need it back?

THAT letter-writer extraordinaire Rudolf Voll, known affectionately as Rude Ole Vole, has spread his net to cover Europe.

For years he has dominated the letters-to-the-editor pages of newspapers in Hongkong and Tokyo, his two main business bases, with his bizarre outpourings.

Here is a classic example of a Voll-ism:

"Oswald Spengler's prediction of the decline of the Occident was, naturally, based on his realisation of the on-going estrangement by Marxist ideas in the West, that promised a permanent handicapping of a nation's economic health due to a natural rift between the have-too-muchs and the too-littles."

Recently, London's *Punch* magazine printed a letter in which Mr Voll was his usual convoluted and puzzling self.

The letter was printed with an editor's note: "Does anyone know what Mr Voll is talking about? All suggestions gratefully received."

Thursday
6
DECEMBER

GOT a Christmas card from Penny Archer at Sunpac Tours and Travel today.

It included a little yellow sticky-back note saying:

"Sign here. And remember to remove the sticker. We don't want to be mentioned in the Lai See column."

A HONGKONG company has just advertised for a "Purchasing executive – lingerie" to deal in "Day and Night Lingeries in the Far East Region".

He or she must have spent three years in lingerie and be familiar with the "technical aspects of lingerie".

We didn't know there were any.

Friday 7 DECEMBER

FASHION firm LiFung Express Ltd of Kowloon has a vacancy that's worth applying for, just for the business card: "Manager — Bottoms."

Candidates need to be fluent in English, says the advertisement, presumably because you have to cope with vast amounts of teasing and innuendo.

You also need to have at least five years experience in ladies' bottoms. That's what it says.

HAD a call from someone today who has been trying to get through to Cathay Pacific cargo reservations department in order to send his cats to the US.

He was put on hold with some music playing, so he switched it to "speaker play" and listened to it while he got on with his work.

He was on hold for three hours.

Is this a record?

Is he now liable to pay royalties to the Performing Rights Society?

Monday 10 DECEMBER

FOREIGN editor Richard Vines went to Dan Ryan's in Pacific Place to have a working lunch with a senior diplomat today.

Despite their having booked under one name, Mr Vines was shown to one table and his guest to another.

"We both ended up dining alone," said Richard. "As I had had a similar experience previously at this restaurant, I wrote to the manager to complain."

His letter said they were going to try dining together at rather closer quarters on Friday, and could the manager PLEASE ensure that they be seated at the same table.

LONDON magazine *Punch* has had a letter from Ms Sandra Dantkin of Vancouver.

"It is with heavy heart that I must inform you that the literary virus known as Rudolf Voll, Hongkong, has infiltrated a relatively venerable publication in North America: *National Geographic.*"

She warns that people must realise "the seriousness and magnitude of this contagion".

Mr Voll, of Hankow Centre, Middle Road, told us that he rather liked the Vancouver lady's portrait of him as a literary virus.

"A literary virus is perhaps of more sinister effect on a nation's mental health than AIDS is on the continued existence of the human race," he said, obscurely.

The weekly magazine *Pyschic News* is looking for a reporter.

Applicants will be pleased to note there are no aptitude tests mentioned.

"We'll KNOW if you are right," says the ad.

We can't help but wonder whether their reporters use telephones and fax machines like we do, or whether they receive their news by closing their eyes and holding hands?

More importantly, can one claim travel expenses for astral projection?

THE Voll controversy continues to escalate. In a

letter to the *Tokyo Weekender*, a Ms Maria Dell Robbia gripes that Mr Voll (described in the letter as 'THAT MAN') had to be made to shut up.

"If I catch Voll down a dark alley in Hiroo [Tokyo's embassy district] I might be tempted to perform acts of physical violence," she writes.

BOFFINS in Yokohama, Japan, have just announced that they can make paper out of sewage pulp. Mr Senji Kaneko, head of the Yokohama City Sewage Bureau's Technology Development Division, said he and other bureau chiefs have been using business cards printed on sewage paper since last summer.

"Nobody notices until I tell them," Mr Kaneko said. "And then the first thing they do is smell the card."

He claims they don't smell of anything.

During the average day, each Yokohama adult produces enough sewage to make four magazine-size sheets of paper, they say.

If the editors of the *South China Morning Post* are getting any funny ideas about cutting printing costs for this column, they can jolly well think again.

Thursday 13 DECEMBER

RUDOLF the red-nosed letter-writer is having a careful Christmas amid fears of persecution. He feels he has achieved the rank of the writer of *The Satanic Verses.*

"I wanted to be in same league as my literary virus idol Salman Rushdie." he said. "Now I have joined that exalted status."

He is keeping a low profile at his Middle Road flat after a growing backlash against his domination of newspaper letters pages around the world.

He reckons the backlash comes from jealous

failed writers of letters-to-the-editor.

"Wish me luck in my darkest hour," he said.

Fortunately, or unfortunately, he has had no success in Iranian publications.

RICHARD Vines caught our elbow in the office.

"It's a funny thing," he said. "But I mentioned my story about being separated from my dining companion to a Swedish woman last night, and she said has had exactly them same experience at Dan Ryan's."

TALKING of happy hang-outs, the RJ Casa Club and Restaurant opens tomorrow at the top of Aberdeen Marina Tower in Shum Wah Road, with a grand party. Wonder where they got the staff, what with the labour shortage?

TODAY dawned bright and clear and lonely diner Richard Vines strolled down to Dan Ryan's at Pacific Place.

He arrived first, and was shown to his table.

The diplomat sidled up almost immediately afterwards, and gave the name under which the table was booked.

Staff told him there was no table booked for him and, bizarrely, asked for his phone number.

Only after complaints did the two gentleman succeed in taking up their implements at the same table.

This is not on. Dan Ryan's really should not take such a proprietorial position over its customers' social lives.

WE see the management of RJ Casa, the new upmarket club, has placed recruitment ads in the newspapers specifying that they want "aggressive" applicants for a number of positions still vacant.

The odd thing is that these vacancies are for waiters, waitresses, bartenders, and a public relations person.

Presumably the waiting staff will use aggression to guide customers: "Hey, ugly, you'd better have the lobster thermidor or things could get really nasty." The PR officer must not only be aggressive but burly with it. The candidate must be male and 6 ft tall or above. This must be so he can take care of people like us.

Monday 17 DECEMBER

WHO says that Hongkong businessmen are devoted to nothing but money? Textile king Dr Henry Li Hong-ling, senior executive at Hongkong Non-Woven Fabric Industrial Co Ltd, has another love in his life: the music of Frank Sinatra.

Dr Li, reading in this newspaper that Ol' Blue Eyes has just turned 75, was so deeply moved that he composed a tribute and sent it to us in the hope that Mr Sinatra would see it.

My dear Mr Frank Sinatra,
Congratulations on your 75th birthday.
I still love your song.
I Left My Heart in San Francisco.
You are Just 75.
And your spirit will carry you to sing on.
You are our Frank Sinatra.

This is touching. Actually, *I Left My Heart in San Francisco* is the signature tune of Tony Bennett (Frank's "city" songs were *New York, New York* and *My Kind of Town).*

But we are not nit-pickers.

Tuesday 18 DECEMBER

IS there somebody out there called Frank of

Shediac Communications Ltd who sent a card to someone called Jon?

If so, did you send him a card showing a individually cut out letters strung together to form the words "mErRy cHrIsTmAs"?

And did it have a yellow stick-on note in it, saying: "If this gets to Lai See and he says it looks like a seasonal %$#@*&¢ ransom note, I'll kick your artistic butt for you at JJ's or wherever you hang out these days"?

Well it did get to us.

And it does look exactly like a %$#@*&¢ ransom note, come to think of it. Poor old Jon.

WE saw an extraordinary ad in a Hongkong-based English language newspaper (not this one) headed: "Application for Alcoholic Licence".

This gave the name of a gentleman in Tai Pei Square, Tsuen Wan, and added:

"If someone discontent this application, he can bring his signature and his reason of discontent to Yeung Uk Road Complex, Tsuen Wan, New Territories, the Alcoholic Council's secretary, from the date which is this advertisement to the date after this day, 14 days."

We think it is a splendid idea that liquor licences in Hongkong should be dispensed by a council of alcoholics.

But does the headline mean that one now needs a licence to be an alcoholic? Shouldn't the committee of the Foreign Correspondents' Club be told?

YOU can get anything you want in Hongkong.

Someone has managed to get access to post office mail between its arrival in Hongkong and delivery to a letterbox.

This we heard from publisher Mike Newlands of Asiavox, who is about to launch a magazine called *East European Opportunities*. He has written off for material from East European embassies.

"I'm getting a huge volume of mail — but every single piece of it has been opened before it gets to me," he said.

MR Newlands today received some innocent Polish material postmarked November 6 — six weeks late.

His letters are kidnapped when they enter Hongkong, held for a few weeks, and then slipped back into the mail.

There is apparently some espionage department in Hongkong which has not realised that the Cold War is over. If it IS secret agents, they are pretty naff bunch. They frequently even forget to reseal the letters.

"I have no idea what to do about it, short of storming the Special Branch offices in Hongkong," he said.

AT the office, we studied the letter in our pigeonhole closely, but it did not seem to have been intercepted by anyone.

It turned out to be *A Song For Hongkong*, specially composed by Frank Sinatra fan and polyester manufacturer Dr Henry Li.

Hongkong, Hongkong, my Hongkong.
A history struggle long
A hand never gone.
Hongkong, Hongkong, my Hongkong
In time of crisis

Will not be in paralysis.
We are a culture of East and West
Expound to the best
We are a mix of North and South
Without any flout
Hongkong will be blessed.
Hongkong a promise land
Trust God in helping hand
Hongkong, Hongkong, my Hongkong.

Mr Li is really good at making polyester products.

WE know two more things about the misguided secret agent who has access to private mail in Hongkong.

1. He can also tune into private phone calls.
2. He is bad-tempered and rather thick.

Mrs Samatha Marmara of Thomas Spencer and Associates, a financial advisory firm, told us that a friend of hers had to call Romania from the phone in her Hongkong-side hotel today. The lady wanted to contact her daughter who is working among the orphans there.

The call went through as expected.

But the secret agent, listening in, obviously got annoyed about this cross-curtain contact going on under his nose.

Throwing caution to the winds, he phoned up the lady concerned.

"Why were you phoning Romania?" he demanded, petulantly. "I want to know who you spoke to? And what was the purpose of the call?"

Phone-buggers never do that in the James Bond films.

TRUCK firm boss Martyn Pegg of Iveco spotted an ad for a lifeguard. "PRODUCTIVITY BONUS," it said.

How does such a thing work in the lifeguard

business? "Surely this can only mean that he has to go around kicking people into the water do he can then save their lives," said a surprised Mr Pegg.

People will do anything for money in Hongkong these days.

MR John Bull of Hongkong-based John Bull Stamps Ltd has just got a Christmas card from China Products' Causeway Bay branch with the following message:

AND GOOD WISHES
AND A
MERRY CHRISTMAS
FOR A
HAPPY NEW YEAR"

He said: "Presumably they are sending these to people who are too drunk to read straight."

DR Marc Faber has been having a little gloat today. Okay, a big gloat. Property has clearly not risen 50 per cent, so he has won his wager.

"Hongkong's real estate agents will NOT be pleased to hear that I will not have to jump down from the Bank of China Tower," he said. "The Bank of China still has plenty of vacancies and therefore, day by day, rentals are gently falling."

As are the spirits of Hongkong estate agents. Merry Christmas.

MR Terry Jenkins, managing director of

National Mutual in Hongkong, has just returned from a business trip to Australia.

"Conditions are getting pretty rough down under and business ethics seem to have gone to the wall," he warned. He showed us a cutting from a Melbourne newspaper about a taipan biting a young man.

"A snake handler was yesterday rushed to hospital after being bitten by a deadly taipan during a presentation for tourists on the Gold Coast. Brent Hitchin, 23, was allowed to leave the Southport Hospital after being given anti-venom."

It does not say which company the taipan was boss of.

Presumably he was driven to the end of his tether by the sinking Aussie stock market, which hit a 33-month low last week.

Mr Jenkins commented: "Fortunately, in Hongkong our taipans still appear to be reasonably pleasant."

But give it time. Simon Murray is known to be a dangerous man, and we would hate to get on the wrong side of Jardines' Nigel Rich.

REAL life conversation overheard at a meeting of senior financial ministers:

Official 1: What a shame about the Uruguay Round talks collapsing.

Official 2: To be honest, I'm not that bothered. Our country doesn't do much trade with Uruguay.

Is there any hope for the world?

THIS year is set to go down in history as The Year The Earth Ran Out of Telephone Numbers, said Luddite Lo. It started with both Hongkong and Shanghai having to add digits to their domestic phone systems. In May, London followed suit. On Tuesday next week, Tokyo will add an extra '3' to all numbers in Tokyo's 03 area code.

This whole thing is becoming ridiculous. You will need a massive 14 digits (a number that would read as 10 trillion) to phone Tokyo.

Yet there are only 6.3 billion (a number with 10 digits) people on earth.

Friday 28 DECEMBER

THE Profit of Doom, Marc Faber, announced a new challenge today.

If the Bank of China Tower is fully let at rents above HK$30 a sq ft by next Christmas Day, he will walk up the entire 70-storey building.

In other words, he is predicting prices will fall almost in half.

"I hate to embarrass real estate agents, because they all have such high intellects and only work for their clients' best interests," he said, piling on the sarcasm with an earth-mover.

What forfeit will he demand from real estate agents if he wins his bet?

"Nothing," he said. "The market will by then have punished them sufficiently."

Saturday 29 DECEMBER

THE global telephone number crisis is set to grow, we were told today by Roger Barlow, international marketing man at Hongkong Telephone.

"Several more cities have plans to change numbering systems soon," he said.

This includes London. Again. "There are serious suggestions that a further digit be added to all UK telephone numbers, including those which changed earlier this year," he said.

WE spent a languid lunch at Grissini mulling over this problem, and came up with an idea.

Lai See would like to propose a once-and-for-all change where everybody in the world gets a new number, perhaps in order of importance.

George Bush could be One, the Queen could be Two, we could be Three (as a thank-you for thinking up the idea), Mr Barlow, Four, and so on up to six billion.

With this system, anyone could call anyone in the world from anywhere in the world by dialling 10 digits or less.

RIGHT. Has everyone got their corporate diaries all lined up for use in the year?

Our favourite is an American one, because Americans have so many holidays.

January is: Human Resources Month; March of Dimes Month; Birth Defects Prevention Month; Careers in Cosmetology Month; Eye Health Care Month; Fibre Focus Month; Hobby Month; Oatmeal Month; Prune Breakfast Month; Soup Month and Volunteer Blood Donor Month.

Hmm. It seems to use that if we celebrate Fibre Focus Month, Oatmeal Month and Prune Breakfast month at the same time, it had also better be Toilet Month.

AT the office, we were most surprised when this popped out from the China Economic Information service:

"BEIJING: A satellite telecommunications network of the People's Bank of China has been put into trial operation.

"Some 800,000 to 1.2 million scores will be settled through the network every day when the bank's branches in all 40 cities joining the network."

Scores settled? By computer? We knew it. This is exactly what we have suspected all year.

JUST as we were writing our last paragraph before leaving for the New Year's Eve party at the FCC, the Lamma Looker called to tip us off that something very strange may be about to happen in Hongkong.

"Did you hear the piece on the BBC World Service in which a tank exporter from Wales was interviewed?" he asked. "No? Well, he said he had customers all over the world for his goods. Including A TANK BUYER from Hongkong."

This was shocking news. Surely it can only be forward planning for 1997. Someone out there is planning a home defence force. Hongkong is not going to take this lying down.

What a thought to end the year with.

FROM THE FILES:
THE SKODA CONTEST

IT quickly became evident to would-be Hongkong Skoda salesman Peter Dutton that no amount of PR about the excellence of his Czechoslovakian-made cars would stem the flow of jokes. "If you can't beat 'em, join 'em," he said, and instituted a competition for readers of the Lai See column to write in with Skoda jokes.

What do you call a patient in a Skoda ambulance?
The deceased.

What's the difference between Arnold Schwarzeneggar's Land Rover and a Skoda?
One's a jeep of hunk, the other's a heap of junk.

What do you call a collision between two Skoda cars?
Czech-mate.

What's in a Skoda tool kit?
A folding bicycle, a spare rubber band, a bottle of valium and the phone number of the Samaritans.

Heard about the new 16 valve Skoda?
It has eight in the engine and eight in the radio.

What do you call an open top Skoda?
A skip (American: a dumpster).

What do you call a Skoda with twin exhausts?
A wheelbarrow.

What's the heated rear window on a Skoda for?
To keep your hands warm while you're pushing it.

What's the difference between a venereal disease, a flat in the London docklands, and a Skoda?
You can eventually get rid of venereal disease and the flat.

What is the difference between a Skoda and Swindon Town Football Club?
It took Swindon Town only 12 days to shift from second to first to third and back again.

What does GTE stand for on a Skoda?
Gets There Eventually.

What do you call a Skoda full of food?
A Lada.

How do you double the price of a Skoda?
Fill it with petrol.

What's the difference between a Skoda and a Jehovah's Witness?
You can shut the door on a Jehovah's Witness.

What do you call a Skoda that starts every other morning?
A miracle.

What do you call a Skoda stretch limo?
A 20 ft container.

What do you call a Skoda four-wheel drive multi-terrain vehicle?
A tractor.

A man walks into a motor spares shop and says: "I'd like a pair of windscreen wipers for my Skoda."
The dealer thinks for a few seconds, then replies: "It's a deal".

A Skoda is at the side of the Tolo Highway, its engine smoking.

A good samaritan called Mr Wong comes along in his Porsche, stops and offers to tow the Skoda into Sha Tin.

They fix a towing rope and set off sedately, but, a mile up the road, a BMW flashes past.

Now Mr Wong is not used to being overtaken by BMWs, so he instinctively puts his foot down.

Later that day, the BMW driver, a Mr Chan,

gets back to his flat in Repulse Bay. He says to his wife: "The most extraordinary thing happened to me today. I was doing 120 mph down the Tolo Highway when a Porsche shot past me at at least 140 mph."

"Nothing unusual in that," said Mrs Chan.

"Agreed," he said. "But right behind him was a Skoda — BLOWING ITS HORN."

Why was a man arrested for cavorting with his girlfriend in the back of a Skoda?
It is illegal to bounce Czechs.

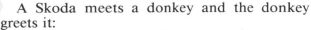

A Skoda meets a donkey and the donkey greets it:
"Hi car, how are you?"
The Skoda replies: "Hi, donkey."
The donkey bursts into tears, saying: "I called you a car. The least you could have done is said: "Hi, horse."

What do you call a joint venture between Fiat and Skoda?
A Fiasko.

Why don't Skodas need car alarms?
Would you steal one?

Two quality control engineers are testing a new Skoda at the production plant in Czechoslovakia.
Engineer one: Put your head out of the window to see if the signal lights work.
Engineer Two: They work. They don't work. They work. They don't work. They work. They don't work. They work. They don't work. They work. They don't work . . .

A Skoda breaks down on the autobahn in Germany. A passer-by tows it to the Mercedes-Benz garage, where the mechanics say they will have to replace the engine.
After the job is done, the Skoda driver heads

off. But he comes back five minutes later and complains that the car runs faster than before, but it runs unevenly, alternately slow and fast.

"Oops. I apologise," says the Benz technician.

He opens the bonnet to reveal a windscreen wiper motor, and flicks the switch from "intermittent" to "on".

What do you call a Skoda with a lawn mower engine?

A Skoda.

It was 5.30 pm on a Friday in Heaven and St Peter was locking up when two figures appeared and asked to be let in.

"Come back on Monday," said St Peter.

"But I'm the Pope," said one. "I just died in my old age."

"I'm a Skoda driver," said the other. "I crashed speeding on the Tuen Mun Highway."

St Peter lets the Skoda driver in and tells the Pope to come back later.

"Why?" asks the Pope.

"We've got loads of Popes but we've never had a Skoda driver who died speeding before."

How do you jump-start a Skoda?

Sneak up quietly behind it and shout: "SCRAPYARD!"

FROM THE FILES:
THE LAI SEE QUIZ

THESE are some questions on the bizarre things that go on in Hongkong and the region, and have been recorded in the Lai See column recently.

Tick your choices as you go through. The answers are at the end.

There are no trick questions.

NOTE: No one has ever been known to get all the answers right.

1. Why did a brain drain survey being completed by the Hongkong Polytechnic take more than a year to complete?

(a) Because no one in Hongkong was interested in emigration.

(b) Because the person in charge emigrated to Canada halfway through the project.

(c) Because the Hongkong Polytechnic was relocated to downtown Vancouver.

2. One of the few bits of good news for Alan Bond in 1989 involved strong consumption of booze, especially among people who put their savings into his shares. One of the most popular was called XXXX. How do you pronounce it?

(a) Forex.

(b) Ex. Ex. Ex. Ex.

(c) Foreign Exchange.

(d) In a way unsuitable for a family publication.

3. Who was Mr Fax Message?

(a) A Hongkong fax junkie who had his name changed by deed poll.

(b) A Pop star.

(c) The name on a cheque sent by a Kowloon-based bank to a Hongkong firm which had communicated with them by fax.

4. Which absentee sent the following message: "Couldn't come today because the chauffeur was ill"?

(a) A stockbroker fantasizing that the boom had returned.

(b) Lai See to the editor of the South China Morning Post.

(c) A child's mother to a junior school on the Peak.

5. A Hongkong property firm was trying to sell a 2,400 sq ft apartment in Mountain Lodge "with a full Aberdeen sunrise" for $4.74 million. This is despite the fact that Aberdeen is on the

west of Hongkong island and the sun rises in the east. What was the reason?

(a) There was a major bout of seismic activity involving Hongkong island.

(b) It was "creative" marketing.

(c) The solar system was temporarily aligned.

(d) The property firm did it with mirrors.

6. Who said: "You give them a really quick freeze, and the shock makes the waste shoot upwards"?

(a) Environment-conscious China Light and Power on a controversial short, sharp shock treatment for litterbugs.

(b) Adman Hans Ebert on his "I'm Pitching In" anti-litter campaign.

(c) Stephen Wong, boss of food firm CP Pokphand, on a method to get rid of the black waste line that runs down the back of prawns.

7. The following correction appeared in the Lai See column: "Yesterday, we told you that AHAFA, formerly FIATA, had become HAFFA, when in fact AHAFA is a member of HAFFA. Aha." What were we talking about?

(a) Vegetarian Food.

(b) Freight forwarders.

(c) Rival military forces in Beirut.

8. From July 1989, holders of foreign currency in the Sudan were:

(a) Given a more favourable exchange rate.

(b) Put to death.

(c) Forced to invest it all in a camel-dung methane plant.

9. "Innovative festival highlights include free photography with a seven-foot-tall walking sausage." What was the festival?

(a) The 3rd annual Giant Perambulatory Foodstuffs show organised by Cahners Expositions at the Hongkong Convention and Exhibition Centre.

(b) A German food festival at Daimaru.

(c) A Japanese celebration called Peripatetic Meat Day.

10. An executive from Jardine Fleming Unit Trusts was overheard saying in Bentley's Seafood Restaurant that there was a Chinese maxim that said: "It is better to have Riches than to have Powers". He was making an oblique reference to what event?

(a) He was looking for a well-paid job with no responsibilities.

(b) He was advising people to sell energy stocks and hoard cash.

(c) A taipan called Rich had taken over from one called Power.

11. Albania announced it was to plug into the Reuters network, allowing it to deal in foreign exchange, bullion and bonds.

What is the currency of Albania?

(a) The Lek.

(b) Leaves of the white mountain fu-fu tree.

(c) The Gumbo Bean.

12. An advertisement in the South China Morning Post said: "Vict s/d: A1 L/hr 20 mns close city Ug. M/wys." What did it mean?

(a) "A Victorian semi-detached house on the A1 motorway 20 minutes from Lahore, close to the city of Ug. Contact woman with Welsh-sounding name."

(b) "A Victorian semi-detached house with pleasant decor, 20 minutes from Heathrow airport, close to City subway station and motorways."

(c) The typesetting machine is broken.

13. What is the real name of Malaysian minister Alias Ali?

(a) John Smith.

(b) That is his real name.

(c) Alias Smith and Jones.

14. The cathedral-like nave of the new Standard Chartered Bank headquarters building features what Hongkong symbol?

(a) A font filled with Holy Water from a spring found underneath the stock exchange.

(b) An altar containing the ashes of the first locally made Filofax.

(c) A stained glass window showing a giant gold mobile telephone.

15. This comes from the biographical data sheet of which man? "His experience includes product tampering, product recall, toxic waste dumps, extortion threats, labour disputes, plant explosions with employee deaths, even a plant site murder."

(a) Death-dealing Triad chief Chiu Sum-fat.

(b) Lai See.

(c) Steve Lyons of Ogilvy and Mather Public Relations.

16. Why did the fax machine produced by Litton Industries Inc of Maryland, US, cost HK$5.2 million?

(a) It was nuclear blast-proof.

(b) It was junk-mail-resistant.

(c) It turned into a long-distance stun gun.

17. The authorities in Vietnam declared that from October 1, 1990, they would confiscate any foriegn cigarettes they found. What did they say they would do with them?

(a) Steam-roll them flat.

(b) Set fire to them.

(c) Force MIAs to smoke them.

18. A Wan Chai businessman who travels frequently to the Middle East was seen wearing a T-shirt with Arab writing on the front during the Gulf War. What was the translation?

(a) I am American and proud of it.

(b) I am not American.

(c) The Ayatollah is a pencil-necked geek.

19. "Spit Police" in Beijing accused several hundred people of spitting on the streets of the city in August 1990. Those who pleaded guilty were fined. Those who insisted they were innocent:
(a) Received written apologies.
(b) Were allowed to spit on the police.
(c) Were fined twice as much.

These are the answers. DON'T PEEK until you have done the quiz.
1. (b)
2. (a)
3. (c)
4. (c)
5. (b)
6. (c)
7. (b)
8. (b)
9. (b)
10. (c)
11. (a)
12. (b)
13. (b)
14. (c)
15. (c)
16. (a)
17. (b)
18. (b)
19. (c)

FROM THE FILES:
THE LAI SEE AWARDS

Most Shocking Case of Animal Abuse:
Reproduced below is a memo that allegedly
went out to IBM branch offices from an engineer
in the United States.
   MOUSE BALLS
   *If a mouse fails to operate or should it perform
erratically, it may need a ball replacement. Because of the delicate nature of this procedure,
replacement of mouse balls should only be at-*

tempted by properly trained personnel.

"Before proceeding, determine the type of mouse balls by examining the underside of the mouse. Domestic balls will be larger and harder than foreign balls. Foreign balls can be replaced using the pop-off method. Domestic balls are replaced using the twist-off method. Mouse balls are not usually static sensitive. However, excessive handling can result in sudden discharge.

"It is recommended that each replacer have a pair of spare balls for maintaining optimum customer satisfaction, and that any customer missing his balls should suspect local personnel of removing these necessary items.

"To re-order, specify one of the following: P/N 33F8462 — Domestic Mouse Balls; P/N 33F8461 — Foreign Mouse Balls."

Worst Targeted Piece of Financial Junk Mail was received by a Hongkong stockbroker in March 1989.

It was from the *Securities Bulletin* of the Hongkong stock exchange, and was addressed to "Mr Dealing Room". The letter inside started "Dear Mr Room . . ."

Worst Addressed Letter to Hongkong was received by Peter Brown of Sopac Management, East Ocean Centre, Granville Road, Tsim Sha Tsui. It was posted in Allentown, Pennsylvania, on June 14, 1990, by AARP Group Health Insurance Program of the Prudential. The address seems to include practically everywhere in the vicinity — except Hongkong.
Seabird Lane
Discovery Bay
Lantau Island
By Macau
Singapore
China.

Best Addressed Letter to Hongkong was received by Clive Goldsworthy, treasurer of the Hongkong branch of the National Australia Bank. It was addressed to:
109 Repulse Bay Road
Hongkong
Hongkong
Just Below China
Turn Left at Japan
And Follow Coast.

Most Pathetic Press Release was received by Lai See in May 1989 from Shing Loong Co.
It said:
"Shing Loong is constantly studying possibilities to expand its activities. From time to time proposals are being considered. Nanyang Finance, Island Finance and Lian Huat Hang Finance are a few such proposals. However, such discussions are still very preliminary."

Least Confident Advertisement was this one:
FAX AND VOICE ON ONE PHONE LINE
No need for a dedicated Fax line.
HK$650.
Tel: XXX XXXX.
Fax: XXX XXXX.
If there is no need for two separate lines, why does he have two lines, one for phone and one for fax?

Most Creative Brochure came from coffee import firm Baco International Co of Tsim Sha Tsui, listing their coffee brands:
DESSERT IMPERIAL
He has a rich aroma with a very sweat after-taste. Dessert coffee has it all. A delicious coffee for sweat-enjoyers.
MARAGIGYE:
Distinguish, as well in his largeality of its beans as his aroma.

GOURMET:
This coffee is light accidulated which give him a specified tasted, pleasant to drink and lightly digestible.
DECAFINE DESSERT:
Although without caffeine, this coffee keeps his full, agreable taste. Specially for people with nerfs.

Most Modest Item on a Hongkong restaurant menu was seen at the Bull and Bear:
"Detectable Chicken".

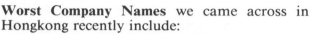

Worst Company Names we came across in Hongkong recently include:
1. Tack Kee Plastic Watch Co.
2. Lee Kee Motor Boat Service.
3. Puking Boutique.
4. Au Choo Medicine Hall.

Special mentions go to Wino Investments and Naughty Boy International Ltd.

Local societies with the broadest potential membership were:
1. Hongkong and Kowloon Mammals Ltd.
2. Hongkong and Kowloon Inhabitants Main Association Ltd.

Other Memorable Company Names in Hongkong, in no particular order, include the following:
Chee Kee Clothing Accessories
Lee Kee Boot Factory
Tack Kee Furniture Co
Hop On Bicycle Co
Dicky Transport Co
Mee Sik Restaurant
Hop On Glass Co
Man Fat Meat Co
Mee Fat Garment Co
Fat Tai Custom Tailors

Sik Kee Tailors
Wing Kee Optical Co
Tong Kee Piano Co
Sher Lee Temple
Peon-Rich Industries
The Dead Disposers Association
Hongkong Kowloon Decorated Paper Box Trade Workers Union
The Hongkong and Kowloon Good Pal's Game Brand Cricket General Association Ltd

Most Publicly Failed Resolution: "I will assiduously avoid a mention in Lai See in 1991," pledged Mr Wesley McDade, public affairs manager of the Securities and Futures Commission, at Christmas 1990. Full details of this pledge were carried in Lai See on January 3, 1991.

Most Brazen Deception Award goes to the Ming Teh Flag Co of Taipei, a Taiwanese firm making United States flags for export to the US in 1989.

After getting the flags through customs, recipients should remove the "Made in Taiwan" sticker, the firm proposed.

"We suggest you cut off the label after you receive the goods, and spend very little cost to mark on the flag your own brand name, and 'Made In USA' labels," it said. "We can offer the labels too," it added helpfully.

Saddest Demise Award goes to Hongkong firm Turns Out All Right Co, which went into liquidation in 1989.

Least Appetising Foodstuff Name goes to Daimaru, for selling a confection labelled Chocolate Negro Balls.

Other recent greats:

Mucos, a Japanese sports drink.

Donkee Basterd Suker, sugar from Amsterdam.

Grated Fanny, canned fish from South America.

Snot, a type of cookie from Japan.

Lai See Hit Parade:

5. *How Can I Be Sure?* by Willy Purves and Sir Kit McMahon.

4. *Pretty Vacant* by Hongkong Land.

3. *Funkytown* by the Singapore Government.

2. *The Call of the Far Away Hills* by the Hongkong public.

1. *Get Back* by the Hongkong Government.

Most Startling Academic Research Project was carried out at the Hongkong Polytechnic on geriatric patients.

"After one year, among the 141 patients studied in the first phase, 37 were dead. The dead and the survived were compared in terms of various aspects of functioning. It was found that, in all five dimensions of functioning, the dead were generally weaker.

"The dead had poorer self-perceived economic conditions. More of them thought that their economic resources were not adequate for them to make ends meet . . .

"The dead also demonstrated a higher level of anxiety than the survived as they found life dull and had more worries . . .

"By and large, fewer dead patients had been able to perform activities to maintain an independent household, eg, moving around, preparing meal, doing household work and washing light clothing.

"Finally, the dead patients had fewer social contacts and more of them were living alone than the survived."

Most Thought-Provoking Computer-Corrected Names, as conjured up by automatic spellcheck programs:

Gordon Wu: *Garcon Woe*
Skoda: *skewed*
Shun Ho: *Shun Ohio*
Dunhill: *Dunghill*
Kumagai: *Kamikazi*
Deng Xiaoping: *Dean Soaping*
Kylie Minogue: *Kilo Monologue*
Omni The Hongkong Hotel: *Omen The Honking Hotel*
Pokfulam: *Potfuls*
Saddam Hussein: *Saddism Hussies*
Wardley: *Waywardly*
Hutchison: *Hatchets*
Jardines; *Sardines*
Swire: *Swipe*
Kowloon Tong: *Colon Town*
Parkview: *Porkpie*
Wanchai: *Wenches*
Nury Vittachi: *Henry Vacuity*

Least Comforting Safety Demonstration: Mr Daniel Akler, a Hongkong-based consultant, settled back in his seat on the morning flight CAAC 319 from Guangzhou to Hongkong on March 18, 1991.

A voice started describing safety procedures on a public address system and a stewardess appeared in an aisle to demonstrate.

Step One: she picked up the life-jacket and tried to undo the buckle. It wouldn't budge.

The voice continued the description and the stewardess looked rather at a loss. Since she couldn't undo the buckle, she couldn't do any of the rest of the operation.

The voice continued to drone.

"She folded up the life-jacket, put it back in its place, and quietly crept away," said Mr Akler.

Clearest Instructions for Airline Passengers were handed out on CAAC:

Please fasten your safety belt properly for your life safe, when planes take off, land and bump.

(The three normal stages of CAAC flights.)

For flight safety, the following items are inherited to carry in the airplane: inflammables, explosives, corrosive poisonous, radioactives.

(There is no information as to how to obtain these if you have not inherited them.)

The washing-room are located the front (middle) and back . . . please don't forget to but the door while you use them.

(We presume that butting the door with one's head is the only way to ensure privacy.)

The 'delay', a popular term of civil aviation is mainly caused by the following two paints.

(Huh?)

If you don't fasten your seatbelt, you may be injured by the strong inertia.

(The strong inertia surely lies somewhere in the CAAC information department.)

Best Hongkong Businessman Joke:

Once upon a time, there was a super-sharp Hongkong businessman who died and went to heaven (yes, yes, but unlikely things do happen in jokes).

"Jo san, God," he says to his Maker. "I had a really good time on earth. But one thing has always puzzled me. Why did you make so many *gweilo?"*

"Well somebody had to pay retail prices," replies God defensively.

Second Best Hongkong Businessman Joke:

Judge: You've been found innocent of the charge of stealing.

Hongkong businessman: Good. Does that means that I can keep the money?

Most Remarkable Stock Market Performance: On Monday, April 22, the Shenzhen share market registered an unprecedented turnover of zero renminbi. Not a single fen of stock was traded, according to the semi-official Hongkong China News Service. And this is in a country where the smallest units of currency are worth about the same as a deutschemark molecule.

Pocket Philosophies: Helen Megan started *Lai See* readers working out minimalist versions of various codes of living:

Taoism: *Bad stuff happens.*

Confucianism: *Confucius say: 'Bad stuff happens.'*

Zen: *What is the sound of bad stuff happening?*

Hinduism: *Hey, this bad stuff has happened before.*

Islam: *Bad stuff is the Will of the Almighty.*

Judaism: *Why does bad stuff always happen to us?*

Catholicism: *Bad stuff happened. But I deserved it.*

Spiritualism: *Bad stuff is just your Uncle Henry mucking around.*

Materialism: *You may have more bad stuff than me, but wait till I go shopping.*

Animism: *We don't need any more bad stuff. Better sacrifice TWO virgins.*

Cannibalism: *That's really bad stuff. But at least we get to eat.*

Atheism: *It may appear to be bad stuff but we don't believe it for a moment.*

Parseeism: *That really is bad stuff. Maybe if we put it on the roof it will go away?*

Jonesism: *Forget about all this bad stuff and just drink your Koolaid.*

Agnosticism: *We don't know if it is bad. We don't even know if he/she/it is even stuff.*

Pessimism: *You think this is bad stuff? This is just the beginning.*

Fundamentalism: *If the Bible says it is bad stuff it IS bad stuff.*

Freudianism: *You're a loony because Oedipus got up to some bad stuff with his mother.*

Surrealism: *Electric giraffe wings.*

Life: The Rules. This series started out as a suggestion by reader Richard Rund that a list of rules of thumb for everyday living would be useful.

□ The life expectancy of a house plant varies inversely with its price and directly with its ugliness.

□ The probability of failure is directly proportional to the number and importance of the people watching the test.

□ The currency of your next travel destination is the one that soars.

□ Deciding to take a taxi causes a dozen other people wanting taxis to materialise.

□ For every five items of post you receive in Mid-Levels, three will be from strangely-named estate agents.

□ Deciding to use an ATM machine will cause the person in front to make 37 inter-account transactions using four cards.

□ A surprise monetary windfall is always accompanied by an unexpected expense of the same amount.

□ If you take something apart and put it back together enough times, eventually you will have two of them.

□ When the plane you are on is late, the plane you are transferring to is on time.

□ The farther from your destination you have to park, the closer the space vacated by the car that pulls away just as you walk up to the door of wherever you are going.

□ The fury engendered by the mis-spelling of a name in a column is in direct ratio to the obscurity of the mentionee.

□ Accomplishing the impossible means the boss will add it to your regular duties.

□ The man who signs the cheques is always out of town.

□ A cheque definitely posted the previous day will take 10 days to arrive in the mailbox.

□ When a stockbroker recommend and investment, one of his friends wants to sell.

□ One-size tights fit no one.

□ The next Christmas card you get is from the person you knocked off your Christmas card list.

□ Never trust a man who looks like he enjoys wearing a suit.

Fifteen Wonderful Country and Western Song Titles:

15. *My Wife Ran Off With My Best Friend — And I Miss Him.*

14. *I Gave Her the Ring and She Gave Me the Finger.*

13. *Flushed From the Bathroom of Your Heart.*

12. *I Gave Up 'Mornin' Honey' and 'Hi There Daddy' For This.*

11. *Drop-Kick Me Jesus, Through the Goal-Posts of Life.*

10. *How Can a Whisky that's Six Years Old Whip a Man that's 32?*

9. *I'd Rather Have a Bottle in Front of Me Than a Frontal Lobotomy.*

8. *From the Gutter to You Ain't Up.*

7. *I've Got Tears in My Ears From Lying in Bed and Crying Over You.*

6. *She Got the Gold Mine and I Got the Shaft.*

5. *I Was a Pushover When She Rolled Off Her Pullover.*

4. *Take Back Your Heart, I Ordered Liver.*

3. *You Pretend I'm Him, and I'll Pretend You're Her.*

2. *You Just Sorta Stepped On My Aorta and Stomped That Sucker Flat.*

1. *Take Your Tongue Out of My Mouth, I'm Kissing You Goodbye.*

GREAT Hongkong conversations:

Bank: Hello.
Caller: Is this the savings account department?
Bank: Sorry, I'll transfer you.
(Beep. Click.)
Bank: Hello.
Caller: Is this the savings account department?
Bank: Sorry, I'll transfer you.
(Beep. Click.)
Bank: Hello.
Caller: What department is this?
Bank: I'm sorry. She's on leave.
Caller: I don't think you understand. I asked what department this was.
Bank: I'M SORRY. SHE'S ON LEAVE.
Is there really a bank savings manager in Hongkong called Dee Partment?

THIS conversation took place between a Hongkong-based German businessman and a receptionist at the Furama Kempinski Hotel.
Caller: Do you have roast goose available at your hotel?
Receptionist: Which room is he in?
Caller: No no. ROAST GOOSE.
Receptionist: YES SIR. What is his ROOM NUMBER?
The businessman told us afterwards: "I should have replied: 'He's probably in the kitchen.'"

BANK technology specialist Marc Nield reserved six tickets on the 6 pm, March 7 jetfoil to Macau by telephone. Then he found he needed only three.

Knowing how tricky bureaucracy can be in Hongkong, he turned up in person at the Far East Jetfoils counter in Shun Tak Centre, Sheung Wan, to explain this difficult concept.

Can't be done, he was told. Company policy says staff cannot accept cancellations from passengers in person. They are only accepted from disembodied voices on the phone.

"If I had a mobile phone I could have just stood there and continued the conversation," he thought.

But he didn't. He spent the next two hours at a phone trying to get through. Eventually, someone picked up the phone.

Mr Nield: I have reserved six tickets for 6 pm on March 7. I want to cancel three of them.

Jetfoils: You must cancel all six and make a new booking for the three you want to keep.

Mr Nield: Okay, fine. (Gives details.)

Jetfoils: What new reservations would you like to make?

Nield: Three tickets for 6 pm on March 7.

Jetfoils: Sorry. 6 pm on March 7 is fully booked.

VISITOR to Hongkong asks if there is a criminal lawyer in town.

Policeman replies: "We think there are several. But we can't prove it."

A RAIN forests preservation campaign was run in Hongkong by Liam Fitzpatrick and his friends. Every HK$500 raised bought one acre of rain forest to be preserved for prosperity.

Liam had a call from a curt and efficient Hongkong businessman:

Caller: I just want to ask you a question about this rain forest thing.

Liam: Sure.

Caller: How can I redevelop my acre of rainforest?

Liam: Redevelop it? Er. It doesn't actually work that way.

Caller: Secondly, what discount do I get if I buy two or more acres?

Liam: Er. I don't think you understand.

Yes, the green movement has a long way to go in Hongkong.

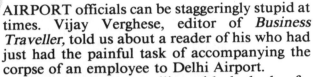

AIRPORT officials can be staggeringly stupid at times. Vijay Verghese, editor of *Business Traveller,* told us about a reader of his who had just had the painful task of accompanying the corpse of an employee to Delhi Airport.

Passenger: I am travelling with the body of a deceased person.

Airport official: Did you kill him?

INDEX

China Economic Information 186
China Travel Service 76
Chinese Wonderful Prescription Co 65
ChinTung International 19
Chiu, Ms 97
Chocolate Negro Balls 203
Chung Kuo 107
Citibank Australia 158, 159
Citicorp Scrimgeour Vickers 142
Clennell, Simon 146
Club Volvo 79, 80, 142
Coca-Cola Indonesia 126
Cohn, Don 90
Goldcorp 165
Convention Centre 10, 71, 81, 137
Corrick, Meg 141
Credit Agricole 151
Crampton, Matthew 56
Crook, Jack 51
Crothall, Geoffrey 77, 95, 144, 152, 157
Crown Motors 70
CSL 3, 5, 16

Dah Wai 33
Daimaru 203
Dan Ryan's 45, 175, 178
Dantkin, Sandra 176
Dataquest 49
Daya Bay 150
DDB Needham 76, 109
Dealing Room, Mr 200
Delaporte, Pierre 100
Deloitte Haskins and Sells 165
Dell Robbia, Maria 177
Deng Xiaoping 142
de Rivaz, Vincent 101
DHL 4
Discovery Bay 163
Dominic's Art Gallery Co 16
Don, Annette 157
Drexel Burnham Lambert 39, 40, 42, 43

Renfrew, Bill 68
Reuter 132, 133
Rich, Nigel 184
Richard, Big Swinging 152, 166, 168
Roberts, Peter 160, 164
Rolex 61, 62
Royal Hongkong Jockey Club 32, 138, 160
Royal Hongkong Police 35, 36
RJ Casa 178
RTHK Radio Three 3
Rushdie, Salman 177

Search and Assessment Services 164
Selway-Swift, Paul 147, 156
Senji Kaneko 177
Shaffer, Bretigne 172
Shandong 91
Shanghai 26, 27, 89
Shediac Communications 180
Shell 36
Shenzhen Stock Market 166, 167, 168, 207
Sheraton 36
Shiel, David 157
Shiel, Miranda 157
Shillingdon, Angus 87
Shing Loong Co 201
Silvercord House 121
Simmonds, Nigel 57, 61, 64
Sin, Yip-keung 17
Sinatra, Frank 179, 181
Sinclair, Kevin 172
Sino Land 18
Skilbeck, Frank 14
Skoda 188-192
Soixante-Neuf, Mr 162
Spurrier, Martin 147
St George's Building 136
St Paul's Hospital 152, 157, 158
Stall, Roy 37
Stanley's Oriental 172
Star Ferry 43

THANKS to all our contributors, who include: David Chappell, Roy Stall, Roberto de Vido, Chris Holmes, Tony Giles, Fred Fredricks, Simon Clennell, Tony Nedderman, Andreas Panayi, Robin Bradbeer, Richard Priest, Richard Rund, Hal Archer, Neil McLaughlin, Paul Brian-Boys, Neil Thomson, Jim Rounik, Ted Powell, Ted Thomas, Roy Munden, Pat Malone, Peter Bentley, Derek Maitland, Dina Temple-Raston, Tai Wai, Jan Altink, Elijah Saatori, Robert Cutler, Tom Marrin, Tom Hall, and others too numerous to mention. Thanks also to the staff of *Business Post;* particularly Geoff Hunt, David Greason, David Mawer and Kenneth Ko.